Inspiring
LIFELONG
READERS

USING INQUIRY TO
ENGAGE LEARNERS
IN GRADES 6–12

JENNIFER
McCARTY
PLUCKER

Solution Tree | Press

a division of
Solution Tree

555 North Morton Street
Bloomington, IN 47404
800.733.6786 (toll free) / 812.336.7700
FAX: 812.336.7790

email: info@SolutionTree.com
SolutionTree.com

Visit **go.SolutionTree.com/literacy** to download the free reproducibles in this book.

Printed in the United States of America

Library of Congress Cataloging-in-Publication Data

Names: McCarty Plucker, Jennifer, author.
Title: Inspiring lifelong readers : using inquiry to engage learners in
    grades 6-12 / Jennifer McCarty Plucker.
Description: Bloomington, IN : Solution Tree Press, [2024] | Includes
    bibliographical references and index.
Identifiers: LCCN 2023022827 (print) | LCCN 2023022828 (ebook) | ISBN
    9781949539875 (paperback) | ISBN 9781949539882 (ebook)
Subjects: LCSH: Inquiry-based learning. | Reading (Secondary) | Reading
    (Middle school) | Book selection. | Motivation in education.
Classification: LCC LB1027.23 .M38 2024 (print) | LCC LB1027.23 (ebook) |
    DDC 371.3--dc23/eng/20230721
LC record available at https://lccn.loc.gov/2023022827
LC ebook record available at https://lccn.loc.gov/2023022828

Solution Tree
Jeffrey C. Jones, CEO
Edmund M. Ackerman, President

Solution Tree Press
President and Publisher: Douglas M. Rife
Associate Publishers: Todd Brakke and Kendra Slayton
Editorial Director: Laurel Hecker
Art Director: Rian Anderson
Copy Chief: Jessi Finn
Senior Production Editor: Christine Hood
Proofreader: Charlotte Jones
Cover and Text Designer: Julie Csizmadia
Acquisitions Editor: Hilary Goff
Assistant Acquisitions Editor: Elijah Oates
Content Development Specialist: Amy Rubenstein
Associate Editor: Sarah Ludwig
Editorial Assistant: Anne Marie Watkins

Acknowledgments

I am a woman of faith—one who does her level best to listen and follow what the Lord wants me to do. Writing this book has been an act of rebellion. I fought Him throughout the whole process. But today, as I write this acknowledgment, I know He is the one I most need to thank. Thank you, God, for pushing me to share my heart and the instructional practices we know empower the identities of readers. Literacy opens doors, and all young people deserve to have those doors open for them.

Thank you to my number-one supporter, my husband Carl. Your encouragement and willingness to pick up all the slack on the home front so I could write is what ensured this book's completion. I love you.

Thank you to my children, Andrew and Ainsley, for sharing me with other people's children and also for allowing me to be your teacher. I love you to the moon and back. Keep reading!

Thank you to my mom, who read to me nightly before tucking me in, showing me the joy that comes from immersing oneself in a story.

Thank you, Dad, for modeling reading my whole life. It still astonishes me thinking about all those Louis L'Amour books you found time to read when I was a child, during what I now know must have been the busiest time of your life.

Thank you to the many, many teachers, colleagues, and coaches who shaped my identity as a reader, learner, and educator. I especially want to thank two of my colleagues, Jessica Crooker and Sarah Papineau, who were my teammates when most of the strategies discussed in this book were proven successful for advancing adolescent readers. Jess and Sarah, you showed me that the most transformative learning occurs when done together.

Thank you to all my former students and young people I have coached, tutored, and mentored. I learned more from you than you from me!

Thank you to the team at Mackin, who insisted I see this book to the finish line.

Finally, thank you to the team at Solution Tree, especially Amy Rubenstein, who patiently nudged me through the entire process, and Christine Hood, whose editorial notes were like a conversation over coffee coaching me to take the manuscript to a higher level.

Solution Tree Press would like to thank the following reviewers:

Kerry Bollman
Instructional Services Coordinator
St. Croix River Education District
Rush City, Minnesota

Jed Kees
Principal
Onalaska Middle School
Onalaska, Wisconsin

Ian Landy
District Principal of Technology
School District 47
Powell River, British Columbia,
    Canada

Kathy Perez
Professor Emerita
Saint Mary's College of California
Moraga, California

Rosalind Poon
Vice Principal
Hugh Boyd Secondary School
Richmond, British Columbia,
    Canada

Jennifer Rasmussen
Literacy Specialist and Instructional
    Service Director
CESA 4
West Salem, Wisconsin

Jose "JoJo" Reyes
Chief Administration Officer
Parlier Unified School District
Parlier, California

Ashley Richey
Mathematics Instructional Coach
East Pointe Elementary School
Greenwood, Arkansas

Kayleigh Steinmetz
English Teacher
Stanley-Boyd High School
Stanley, Wisconsin

Emily Terry
English Teacher
Kinard Middle School
Fort Collins, Colorado

Visit **go.SolutionTree.com/literacy** to download
the free reproducibles in this book.

Table of Contents

Reproducibles are in italics.

About the Author

Jennifer McCarty Plucker, EdD, is the director of learning and development and a literacy consultant at Mackin Educational Resources in Burnsville, Minnesota.

Dr. Plucker has spent more than twenty years in public education as an English teacher, reading specialist, speech coach, teaching and learning specialist, and district administrator. Her doctoral research focused on student engagement and motivation in literacy. Her current work with educators is grounded in an inquiry approach that puts students in the driver's seat of their learning. She supports educators in implementing inquiry in the classroom, redesigning the English language arts (ELA) curriculum to support student ownership, implementing practices to motivate and engage readers, developing secondary literacy intervention programs, and supporting school communities in developing a culture of literacy. Dr. Plucker has served as an adjunct instructor for Hamline University in Saint Paul; Augsburg College in Minneapolis; and Saint Mary's University in Winona, Minnesota. Dr. Plucker also currently serves on the Eastview Community Foundation Board and supports young people as a leadership development manager for Chick-fil-A Apple Valley.

Dr. Plucker is a past president of the Minnesota Reading Association, where she was recognized as a celebrated literacy leader. The literacy intervention program Dr. Plucker implemented for ninth graders at Eastview High School in Apple Valley, Minnesota, was recognized by the International Literacy Association. Dr. Plucker was also awarded an Alumni Success Award from Argosy University for her doctoral research and leadership in literacy. Dr. Plucker highlighted her literacy intervention for adolescents in an article in the Association for Supervision and Curriculum Development's *Educational Leadership* called "Baiting the Reading Hook" (October, 2010).

Dr. Plucker holds a bachelor's degree in secondary English and speech and theater education from Minnesota State University, Moorhead; a master's degree in educational leadership from Saint Mary's University; a K–12 reading license from Hamline University; and a K–12 administrative license from Saint Thomas University. She received her doctorate in educational leadership with a focus on adolescent literacy from Argosy University, Twin Cities.

To learn more about Dr. Plucker's work, visit www.mackinlearning.com or follow her @jenplucker on X (formerly Twitter).

To book Jennifer McCarty Plucker for professional development, contact pd@SolutionTree.com.

Introduction

In 2007, I was working on a project for a quantitative research class I was taking for my doctoral degree. I was convinced there were students in my on-level, tenth-grade English class who not only were not reading at grade level but might be reading far below grade level. In addition, they were not receiving any other services through special education, tutoring, or English learner programming. My hunch turned out to be correct. When a student attends a high school where the mean percentile on a norm-referenced standardized reading test is the 70th percentile, and that student is barely hanging on in the 10th–20th percentile, they find sophisticated ways to cope.

I discovered that some of the students had strong support at home to help them slog through the whole-class novels, history, science, and wellness textbooks, all of which were written at college levels. Others had given up on being a "scholar" and found nonacademic ways to identify themselves as successful, whether it was through being the captain of a sports team, a supervisor at an area quick-service restaurant, or a nationally recognized traveling soccer player.

The informal study I did for my class was an affirmation of my decision to pursue a K–12 reading license, and eventually a doctorate, in educational leadership with an emphasis in adolescent literacy. I realized that my students' needs were not being met, and I had a moral responsibility to help them. The K–12 reading license provided me with the knowledge and skills to support students who hadn't yet mastered emergent reading skills.

The catalyst for this decision, however, was a parent-teacher conference forever burned into my memory. (Throughout this book, I will share stories about teachers and students I have worked with. To protect their privacy, I use pseudonyms.) In this conference, I was telling a parent that her son, Brady, was struggling in my class because I did not think he was comprehending the book *Of Mice and Men* (Steinbeck, 1937). Brady told me he read the book but just didn't get it. I saw Brady attempting to read during class; he was trying. I just did not think he understood the material. Brady's mother's response to what I thought was insightful feedback was not what I expected. Thinking back, I am not sure what I expected her to say. Maybe, "OK, we'll work together on it at home more," or "Do you think he should be tested for special education?" or "Yes, reading just isn't a strength for Brady." Instead, she responded with the most perfect, appropriate response. She said, "What are you going to do about that?" And with that one sentence, I was rendered speechless.

It was early in my teaching career. I felt like I had great activities to bring books to life. I shared all sorts of insights I had gleaned from the many times I had read the book I was teaching at the time. I would offer to have a paraprofessional read the class novel aloud for any interested students, nudging some of those with individualized education programs (IEPs) to take her up on it. But I hadn't even considered what my role was in helping tenth graders comprehend. Didn't they learn that in elementary school? I am not a reading teacher. I teach literature, rhetoric, writing, public speaking, and interpersonal communication.

So, I responded to Brady's mother, "I'm not sure, but I am going to try to figure it out." I wish I could say Brady and I figured it out. But the truth is, I just discovered that I really didn't have the tools to help him. I certainly did all I could with what I knew; but ultimately, I was going to need to go back to school and learn.

I started noticing my colleagues refer to students who were struggling to make their way through the tough texts as "lazy," "unmotivated," or even "low IQ" students. I don't think they meant it as judgmental or realized how derogatory such sentiments were. I think they wanted a reason why these students were not finding success in their classes. The cringe in the pit of my stomach motivated me to embark on a journey to advance adolescent readers in my classes. I realized that my colleagues and I could no longer excuse students' lack of reading success and engagement. We needed to do something. It's never too late to support students in their literacy growth.

STORIES FROM THE FIELD

It is the week before school starts, and we are gathered for freshman orientation, that exciting evening when energy flows throughout the building. Upperclassmen abound to guide new students through the hallways, recruit them into their activities, and show them school spirit. We start with an assembly in the gym. The band plays, the step team performs, and the cheerleaders teach all the cheers ninth graders need to know to be ready for the pep fest on the first day of school. After our principal releases students and families, they walk their schedule and briefly meet each of their teachers. I race up to my room to beat the students there and await my new crew. It is the same every year, and I am ready.

Students arrive at a class on their schedule called Academic Literacy, having not signed up for it and dreading it. This course is for students identified as needing an extra dose of literacy instruction. These students have struggled with reading, standardized exams, and often school in general for years. Many students' hoods are up, heads are down, and greetings are inaudible. I get it. If I didn't swim well, didn't like to swim, and now have swimming on my schedule every day, I wouldn't go bounding in to meet my teacher. So, I gently nudge them by saying, "Take a look around the room. Find a place where you might want to cozy up with a book next week."

The room is filled with comfy places to sit, bookshelves are packed with engaging young adult books, and walls are painted in a warm and inviting color. This room does look different from the stark white, industrial classrooms students will visit the rest of the day. I smile. I ask nonthreatening questions to begin to get to know them. I assure them we are going to have fun in this class. I ask them to trust me; I tell them that they will also grow as readers, writers, and communicators along the way.

Launching Academic Literacy

Fortunately, at the same time I was making my own personal discoveries and setting a new resolve, my school district was embarking on its study of secondary literacy. The district initiative shined a spotlight on many areas we could improve for adolescent literacy, including leadership, core instruction, literacy intervention, data analysis, and resources used to advance readers. This focus allowed for collective resolve, leadership, and funding, which all contributed to my learning.

Eventually, the district saw great success in the literacy intervention program a few of the teachers on the committee, including myself, developed—called Academic Literacy. Academic Literacy began as a class for ninth graders at my high school; after a few successful years, I got the opportunity to lead the program across all the middle and high schools in our district. We saw gains for all students in literacy, whether in reading support courses, on-level English classes, or advanced programming.

At the beginning of the process, I set out to discover which ninth graders were reading below and far below their peers. In my school, that meant these students, if average according to national norms (50th percentile), would still be below their peers (70th percentile). Once I was able to see clearly, from a triangulation of reading data, that our high school had a substantial number of students reading below grade level and a group (15 percent of the ninth-grade class) in the 1st–25th percentile, I knew I needed to do something. Our high school did triage for one year while a team of reading specialists, English teachers, administrators, and special education teachers from our high school began a more comprehensive review of the literature on what works for adolescents. While we didn't want to wait a whole school year, we knew that budgeting for the following school year would begin in October, so we needed to have a strong vision for intervention programming that science was telling us would really work.

When practices are grounded in the principles of adolescent literacy, complex literacy learning, motivation, and engagement, students' literacy skills can advance rapidly. A visionary team of educators who are willing to home-grow a custom intervention program steeped in evidence and research, and designed with their students in mind, can see students' literacy lives flourish. While we were excited to pilot Academic Literacy, the students were a bit reluctant.

This intervention program was developed based on the research for engaging and advancing readers, and it proved successful, showing reading growth at three or four times the rate of students' on-level peers (Plucker, 2010).

Beyond the readers for whom we built an intentional intervention program, we discovered we had many more skilled readers who were not reading. We had students who were reluctant, avoidant, or resistant. We also had students who were ravenous readers but didn't necessarily see themselves as readers. A team of educators across the district took what it learned from the Academic Literacy program and tried out the program in many of our middle school and high school English language arts (ELA) classes, middle school science and social studies classes, and even in an advanced placement (AP) class. We found the principles and practices used in the Academic Literacy program, and shared throughout this book, work for all kinds of learners.

Before exploring specific literacy strategies, let's examine the literacy challenges and demands facing students, which compete with the attention we know must be placed on their reading, writing, and speaking skills.

Facing Challenges in Literacy

Challenges abound for educators and learners when it comes to advancing literacy skills. Several assessments confirm the fact that high school students are not graduating high school with the literacy skills necessary for college and careers. Elizabeth Birr Moje, Rhonda L. Richetta, Sonja B. Santelises, and David M. Steiner (2017) tell us, "Despite the increased focus on early literacy instruction sparked by No Child Left Behind, millions of adolescents still struggle with low literacy skills." The National Assessment of Educational Progress (NAEP; The Nation's Report Card, 2023) results showed persistent declines in reading for both fourth and eighth graders. While the reading scores have remained flat for years, in 2020 they dropped pretty much across the board.

According to NAEP (The Nation's Report Card, 2023):

> The 2023 average scores in reading declined compared to 2020 for many student groups reported by NAEP; for example, scores were lower for both male and female 13-year-olds, for students eligible and not eligible for the National School Lunch Program (NSLP), and for students attending schools in the Northeast and the Midwest regions.

The reality of these statistics is likely apparent for literacy educators and students everywhere. Students need a sense of urgency to create conditions to advance their skills.

University of Maryland literacy expert Peter Afflerbach attributes this decline to the pervasive belief that students learn to read in grades kindergarten through three and then "read to learn" from fourth grade forward (as cited in Green & Goldstein, 2019). This view has led to elementary students spending their time reading short passages rather than being challenged with longer, thematically rich books. Afflerbach asserts the eighth-grade results emphasize that adolescents do not have the comprehension skills necessary to tackle complex texts (as cited in Green & Goldstein, 2019).

The need for critical thinking and deep comprehension skills is further highlighted in the World Economic Forum's (2023) *Future of Jobs Report 2023*. This report explains that the demand for skills in the 2023 job force will move well beyond the basics of reading and writing and call for analytical thinking, creative thinking, resilience, flexibility, agility, motivation, curiosity, life-long literacy, and more (World Economic Forum, 2023). If students are struggling to meet basic proficiency on the NAEP reading assessment, how might we tackle the challenge of preparing our students for future jobs?

Harvard literacy expert Catherine Snow advises that educators integrate foundational literacy skills into inquiry lessons that excite students. Intrinsically motivating tasks revolving around students' interests drive them back to more texts for information (as cited in Green & Goldstein, 2019). As educators, we need to position reading and writing as tools for learning and inquiry if we want to address these challenges with proficiency. To do that effectively, we also need to understand the demands for students' attention and use that information to inform planning and instruction.

STORIES FROM THE FIELD

Teaching sophomores at a large comprehensive high school meant I would have upward of thirty-six students per class and often four sections. Getting to know more than 140 students on a personal level so I could individualize instruction meant I needed to invest in activities in which students' reflections revealed not only who they are but also their understanding of instructional goals. I had little time for icebreakers and gimmicky games. Instead, I relied on fun ways to engage students in ELA content while also building relationships, rapport, and connections.

On the first day of tenth-grade English, I presented my students with the following text from Kelly Gallagher's *Teaching Adolescent Writers* (2006):

> You're standing in a large field minding your own business when you hear rumbling sounds in the distance . . . you wonder if it is thunder you hear approaching. Because it's a beautiful cloudless day, you dismiss this notion. . . . Instantly, you become panicked because at that exact moment it dawns on you that the rumbling you're hearing is the sound of hundreds of wild bulls stampeding over the ridge. . . . They are clearly faster than you, and there is no time to escape. What should you do? Survival experts recommend only one of the following actions:
>
> A. Lying down and curling up, covering your head with your arms
>
> B. Running directly at the bulls, screaming wildly and flailing your arms in an attempt to scare them in another direction
>
> C. Turning and running like heck in the same direction the bulls are running (even though you know you can't outrun them)
>
> D. Standing completely still; they will see you and run around you
>
> E. Screaming bad words at your parent(s) for insisting on a back-to-nature vacation in Wyoming (pp. 1–2)

Students first reflect on this scenario and write why they chose their response. We have fun exploring each person's answer. I like to use the four corners (and the middle of the room) method to get a quick visual of what each student chose. I direct them, "Go to the back right corner of the room if you chose A, go to the back left if you chose B," and so on. I let students talk and defend their choices. They have a chance to change their mind before the final answer is revealed. (If you are curious about the final answer, be sure to check out Gallagher's 2006 book *Teaching Adolescent Writers*.)

Students find their way back to their seats, and I share the literacy data to show that they are living in the information age, and literacy is stampeding upon them at a relentless speed. The goal of the activity is to help students see their role in being prepared for and engaging in the flood of text that surrounds them. We reflect on how we will engage in class to be best prepared to navigate this stampede.

The scientific benefits of reading books in print include deeper comprehension, especially with expository texts, and greater efficiency because readers can maintain attention longer due to fewer distractions than when reading on screens (Clinton-Lisell, 2019). Students are expected to engage with an increased volume of text online, as well. Therefore, educators must consider supporting student skills in navigating digital texts.

Let's also not forget that the inundation of information for adolescents is overwhelming. Students (well, really most of us) spend hours every day staring at a screen. Some of that time is spent doing meaningful reading, but much of it is scrolling, often mindlessly, through social media. Though our students are digital natives, they often live as "tech comfy," not "tech savvy" (Maiers, 2012). They plan and relax with technology, but they don't always know how to work with it. It is the responsibility of schools and parents to help students become sophisticated "info-sumers, critical thinkers, and savvy participants in digital space" (Maiers, 2012). This means we need to intentionally teach students all the great digital tools available within their eReader or available to them when they are reading articles, PDFs, and more online.

Increasing Demands for Readers' Attention

Gaining students' attention is particularly challenging for a variety of reasons. Teens are actively pursuing friendships, engaging with technology many hours a day, completing academic work, and participating in co-curricular, employment, or other after-school activities. Additionally, adolescents are dealing with increased levels of stress and anxiety (Warren, 2023). As educators, we need to understand the variables that compete with getting students interested in reading. Whether we choose to assign reading with print or digital texts, we do need to acknowledge the challenges for readers' attention so we can be intentional about supporting them in actually engaging with and comprehending the reading they are doing each day.

Before the COVID-19 pandemic, a 2018 American Psychological Association (APA) survey revealed that teens reported higher levels of anxiety and depression than all other age groups (as cited in Divecha, 2019). During the pandemic, the news remained grim. A Centers for Disease Control and Prevention (CDC) report published in 2022 revealed that "more than a third (37%) of high school students reported they experienced poor mental health during the COVID-19 pandemic, and 44% reported they persistently felt sad or hopeless." And data from the annual State of Pediatric Mental Health in America 2023 report show that youth are still suffering (Warren, 2023). It's no surprise that when students are experiencing stress, it can be especially difficult to engage with reading.

So, if educators want to support stressed-out students, one easy way to do that is to provide time for students to read during school hours. The data are clear that students are not reading enough, so to reverse the damage, we have a responsibility to ensure students begin to devote time to reading again. Between 1984 and 2020, the percentage of fourth graders reading for fun almost every day declined from 54 percent to 42 percent. Declines are evident for thirteen- and seventeen-year-olds as well. The percentage of students who never or hardly ever read rose from 9 percent to 16 percent for U.S. nine-year-olds, and from under 10 percent to almost 30 percent for both thirteen- and seventeen-year-olds (Schaeffer, 2021).

When I interviewed some ninth graders for my doctoral research, one of the questions I would ask is "Do you consider yourself a reader?" Almost all my students said *no*. When I pressed, they often replied by saying things like, "I am a snowboarder," "I am a football player," or "I dance." I realized that my students saw reading as a hobby. Of course they did. Don't most people often refer to it as a hobby? Many students thought of readers as those who frequented the library or used free time in class, at lunch, or while waiting for their ride with their nose in a book. Yes, of course, these are readers. But many more readers don't fit this stereotype. So, I set out to redefine literacy in the hopes of shifting students' views. I wanted them to embrace the identity of reader and scholar in addition to all their other passions. And I wanted them to see that literacy lived within their passions.

The ninth graders in the Academic Literacy program, the tenth graders in my on-level English and Speech 10 course, and the seniors in my advanced public speaking class all went on a journey with me to transform our learning environments into one where we had a community of readers. Since that time of experimentation, action research, and innovation, I have had the opportunity to come alongside many passionate educators as they embarked on their own quests for student acceleration and engagement in literacy. This book aims to share the ways you, too, can join us on this journey.

About This Book

While this book is primarily written for middle and high school reading and ELA teachers, the strategies presented can be beneficial across grades K–12 and into other content areas as well. In my current literacy consulting, I also have seen success with the strategies used in high school career and technical education courses, middle school science classes, secondary social studies, and even with a group of kindergartners in Pennsylvania, showing that the principles have broad application.

This introduction sets the stage by exploring the catalyst for change in one high school, which resulted in accelerated literacy growth and improved student ownership of learning. We examined the realities for our adolescent readers, including the demands for their attention, their challenges with deep comprehension, and their misconceptions about defining a *reader* and *text*.

Students persist in difficult learning when they feel like they belong to a community (Bowen, 2021). The first three chapters of this book focus primarily on building a culture where students are poised for progress. Chapter 1 explores the importance of building a community of readers, writers, communicators, and thinkers. This community ensures that students know their value and their role and that their presence is critical to the growth of each individual. Students learn how high expectations and high support lead to confidence and achievement. Chapter 2 discusses how to create a "book flood" and support students in embracing this flood and using it for their enjoyment and achievement (Gallagher, 2009). Students deserve to see themselves in the text; therefore, we must prioritize an inclusive classroom library. Students are most engaged and motivated to persevere with challenging tasks when they feel they are in the driver's seat. Chapter 3 explores how inquiry is a vehicle for both literacy growth as well as engagement.

While building a supportive culture is essential, structure also is necessary. For a literacy or ELA program not guided by a computer program or a script to work, it is critical that educators and learners structure class time proactively to preserve and utilize every instructional minute. Therefore, chapter 4 examines the workshop framework—a brilliant structure for individualized and collaborative learning— and the adjustments necessary for secondary students. As students get older, the gap widens, and the time educators have available to help students catch up to their peers diminishes. Therefore, every action and decision must be tied to accelerated growth. Chapter 5 offers both the research and practical strategies for applying intentional instruction to achieve the goal of getting students as far as possible as fast as possible on their literacy journey.

So often, students who struggle with reading feel defeated, dependent, and discouraged. These students need to be celebrated authentically and frequently to stay engaged so they can experience feeling energized, equipped, and encouraged. Chapter 6 differentiates celebration from prizes and other extrinsic rewards, so it can be a tool for the development of intrinsic motivation.

When reviewing the growing body of research around adolescents, the themes of literacy, motivation, engagement, and accelerated learning emerge. These themes are woven throughout the book and include examples and opportunities for practical application. I also feature Stories From the Field (anecdotes and narratives from my own classroom experiences), reproducible resources and templates you can use or remix to implement activities and strategies, and ideas to get you started.

Conclusion

As you read this text, know that you can read it from start to finish or begin in the chapters that speak to the needs you are experiencing right now. There is no step-by-step manual that will work to transform your classroom. In my experience coaching teams of educators to use an inquiry approach to develop life-long readers, teachers were already implementing many of the principles you will see in this book. What they needed was affirmation and guidance. I hope this book serves as that for you—affirmation that you already bring passion, brilliance, and energy to your craft, and guidance for how you might make some adjustments to your instruction to achieve the goal of getting young people to love reading (again)!

CHAPTER 1

Building a Community of Readers, Writers, Communicators, and Thinkers

No two readers are alike. I had a humbling experience with a student at the start of one school year. I have always been very protective of the time I have with readers and want to ensure they have books they are interested in reading. I give students interest inventories, book talks, and offer "book speed dating," which is when students spend just a few minutes with a book, record some first impressions, and then move to the next book (Ullmer, 2023). I also gather books I think individual students will be interested in and pile them on their desks when they walk into my room. I try to do this by the third day of school if I can.

This strategy usually works; however, it didn't work with one student. This student, Devon, reminded me of a student I had the previous year, Ricky. Devon and Ricky both loved basketball, listened to similar music, and dressed almost identically. So, I went to Ricky's list of favorite books, pulled five or six of them, and placed them on Devon's desk. I was confident he would choose one and start reading.

Instead, to my surprise, he approached me and said, "Dr. McCarty, why do you think I want to read books about drugs and gangs? Or steroid use in football? Or basketball?" I was impressed that he would feel comfortable and confident to ask me this. And then I needed to humble myself.

"Devon, you remind me of a student I had last year, so I gave you books he enjoyed. In my hurry to get books in your hands, I made assumptions about who you are. I'm sorry! What do you want to read about?"

Thankfully, Devon extended me some grace and opened up about wanting to read stories about people who had experienced child abuse and survived. So, I placed *A Child Called "It"* (Pelzer, 1995) and *Three Little Words* (Rhodes-Courter, 2008) on his desk. He picked up *A Child Called "It"* and was engrossed in minutes. I learned a valuable lesson that day. I needed to not be in such a hurry. Had Devon not had the courage to talk to me, he may have spent the year wondering how else I might stereotype him or what else I would assume about him without genuinely getting to know him. I am thankful for the experience, however embarrassing, because it serves as a continual reminder to take the time to get to know learners in my classes. This time invested early pays dividends all year long.

If you are like me, you too may have found yourself making assumptions about students and perhaps not even realizing how those conclusions can affect the reader. In this chapter, we will explore some practical ways to get to know individual students in your classes and how to be intentional in building relationships and creating a community of readers, writers, and thinkers.

Investing in Student Relationships and Community Building

Productive and positive teacher-learner relationships have been long verified in the research community for positive educational outcomes (Zheng, 2022). Specifically, when we are warm, can empathize with our students, and show genuine care, students tend to perform better academically. In *The Teacher You Want to Be* (Glover & Keene, 2015), a powerful collection of essays by thought leaders in education, this sentiment articulates the lens through which educators can view learners: "We believe educators should have a positive and expectant view of children, with an understanding that children enter school with personal histories and particular strengths that teachers should recognize and use as the foundation for working with them" (p. xix). Students do not come as empty vessels; they come with incredible experiences, gifts, and strengths that can and will contribute to the classroom community.

The learner-centered classroom, not to be confused with a child-centered classroom, fosters a focus on the learner and the learning. The latter is only focused on the learner. Educators can build relationships and community while simultaneously helping students acquire content. For this to occur, educators need to remember that each learner is unique, learning is a constructive process occurring best in positive environments, and learning happens naturally (McCombs & Whisler, 1997).

This is important to consider when thinking about how to launch the year with your readers, writers, thinkers, and communicators. We could spend time having students introduce themselves, talk about their summers, and share their hobbies, passions, and interests. Or we could dive right into becoming better readers and writers and, through the process, encourage learners to reveal their interests. When students, particularly low-income students, have positive relationships with teachers, they will be more confident, get along better with their peers, and be able to take on increasingly difficult texts (Zheng, 2022).

To build strong relationships with students, we have to show them we trust them (Burns, 2022). And we can foster student agency by putting them in the driver's seat of their own learning. An inquiry approach to instruction allows the teacher to step aside and give students that ownership. You will find a more detailed examination of the inquiry approach in chapter 3 (page 65); however, the following section will introduce the concept.

Using the Inquiry Approach to Instruction

Learning occurs naturally when educators take an inquiry approach to instruction (Spencer & Juliani (2017). Inquiry is about capitalizing on students' curiosity instead of a scripted curriculum. Instead of sitting in desks and rows, group students for the purposes of collaborating, making choices, using their voices to contribute to the learning, and taking responsibility for their learning. An inquiry approach to learning promotes engagement, provides authentic opportunities for differentiation, and fosters a community of readers, writers, speakers, and thinkers (Daniels, 2017). Critical components of inquiry instruction include questions for student investigations, immersion into print and digital texts for research, numerous opportunities for student choice, and an authentic opportunity for students to teach others what they have learned (Harvey & Daniels, 2015).

For example, suppose you are introducing the concept of *literary devices* in the ELA classroom. You start by writing the word *onomatopoeia* on the whiteboard, and then pass out a blank sticky note to each student as they enter the classroom.

Tell students, "On your sticky note, write either what you think the word on the board means or give an example."

This activates prior knowledge and transitions students into the day's work. Some students will already know that *onomatopoeia* is the formation of a word making the sound associated with the word, such as *splat*, *bam*, or *sizzle*. Other students will not know the definition yet. Have some students share their ideas with a partner and the whole group.

Next, invite curiosity into the classroom. You might say, "I wonder how authors use onomatopoeia and other literary devices in their writing . . . and why."

Rather than having students answer you, give them a list of more literary devices and definitions and a set of picture books that include literary devices.

Figure 1.1 shows a list of books you can use to send students on a scavenger hunt not only to find examples of literary devices, but also to record how the author uses them and why they think the author chose to employ these devices.

Literary Devices	Texts for Literary Device Scavenger Hunt
Onomatopoeia: The formation of a word makes the sound associated with the word; it sounds like what it means.	*Barnacle Is Bored* by Jonathan Fenske (2016)
	The Day the Crayons Came Home by Drew Daywalt (2015)
Analogy: Comparing two unlike things to show equal weight; often follows the structure of *A is to B as C is to D.*	*It's So Quiet: A Not-Quite-Going-to-Bed Book* by Sherri Duskey Rinker (2021)
Personification: Giving human characteristics to nonhuman objects or concepts.	*The Moon Is a Silver Pond, The Sun Is a Peach* by Sara Cassidy (2022)
	My Monster Moofy by Annie Watson (2021)
Allusion: Making reference to a commonly known piece of literature, art, film, television show, or music.	*Old MacDonald Had a Boat* by Steve Goetz (2018)
Pun: Play on words for humor, often playing on multiple definitions of a word.	*Seaside Stroll* by Charles Trevino (2021)
	Today I Am a River by Kate Coombs (2023)
Juxtaposition: Putting contrasting ideas together.	*The Truth About My Unbelievable Summer* by Davide Cali (2016)
Hyperbole: Overly exaggerating.	*Waterson* by Tim McCanna (2017)
Alliteration: Stringing words together that start with the same first letter.	

Figure 1.1: Literary device scavenger hunt.

A principal tenet of inquiry is the development of more questions, so encourage students to record their wonderings throughout the scavenger hunt. At the end of the hour, compile your findings and dialogue with students about whether what they found fits the definitions. Be careful not to tell students their findings are wrong. Instead, you are growing your understanding together, and misconceptions are a welcome part of the learning process. This is just one simple example of how inquiry can create curiosity, place learning on students' shoulders, and provide opportunities for building trust.

Sometimes we, as educators, feel pressured to get the year started by immediately jumping into the content. Or, we feel like we need to take some time to engage in icebreakers, get-to-know-you activities, and discussions about rules and policies. With inquiry-based instruction, we can jump right into the content and weave our icebreakers and setup procedures together all at once. With that in mind, let's explore some practical and authentic ways to build productive relationships and structure in our classroom communities.

Building a Structured Classroom Community

Students will more easily engage in the inquiry process when they feel like they have a predictable routine. As you work to build trust, get students to open up to one another, and encourage students to take the risks necessary for inquiry work, first provide some structure to the classroom. I recommend following a workshop framework, which I discuss in more detail in chapter 4 (page 109).

In *So What Do They Really Know?*, Cris Tovani (2011) defines the workshop approach as a predictable routine in which students know the class period begins with an opening and minilesson as a whole group and then moves into work time with opportunities for check-ins, or what Tovani refers to as *catch-and-release times*. Finally, every class ends with the whole group coming back together to debrief. Students need considerable time to engage in inquiry through reading, writing, collaborating, and thinking. They need opportunities to share their thinking, hear reactions, and respond to new ideas. During work time, instructors can pull small groups for guided practice, confer one on one with students, and roam the room making careful observations to guide further teaching.

When my colleagues and I introduced the workshop framework to students, we simplified it by letting them know we would start together as a whole group; students then would move into guided practice—which could be independent or in small groups—and we always ended together back in the large group. I was pleasantly surprised at how effective it was to provide this predictable structure for students each day. I think we forget how much cognitive and emotional currency is wasted as students transition from class to class. The workshop framework saves some of that currency.

Providing time during class for independent reading was a priority for our reading and ELA classes. With a workshop framework in place, there was a guaranteed time set aside each day for independent or small-group practice. This guided practice time could be used for students to read independently; however, before I could consider providing class time for reading, I needed to help students be successful in sustaining their attention while reading on their own.

I start by teaching students to notice and name the distractions that kept them from sustaining their attention on reading. Rather than policing student behavior during reading time, I asked students to journal and record any time their mind wandered, their focus waned, or they had to go back and reread. I asked them to consider what caused the distraction and how quickly they could redirect their attention back to the reading or task at hand.

Stories From the Field

Working with the ninth graders in the Academic Literacy program, I learned quickly that my type-A personality was going to have to flex. I couldn't expect students to be compliant, follow instructions the first time I gave them, or provide me with respect from the get-go just because I was their teacher. I didn't want to lower my expectations, but I needed to meet these students where they were. So, I started keeping an observation chart. What were the behaviors I was seeing that seemed to get in the way of the learning we were doing? One of my colleagues did the same in her class.

When we compared notes, we started to see some patterns. We decided that instead of focusing on the negative aspects of students' behavior, we would study, compile, and characterize the behaviors to better understand them. In that meeting, we created our "cast of characters." Meet them here. Have you met some of these students yourself (Plucker, 2009)?

Tardy Tracy—Isn't there a clock on your cell phone?

Absent Ahmad—MIA . . . a lot.

Bobby Belligerent—The answer is always *no*!

Jack Jokester—Lots of jokes, often inappropriate

Sleepy, Dopey, Droopy . . . Wait, are those dwarves?

Sneezy Sofia—Frequent visits to Nurse Peggy

Charlie Charmer—Everybody's buddy

Forgetful Fay—No pencil, no notebook, no problem

Billy Bladder—Suspiciously well-hydrated

Celine Cell—So many texts, so little time

Messy Malik—Something could be living in that backpack

I-Couldn't-Care-Less Chris—Surprisingly indifferent about everything

This activity allowed us to have a little fun with the challenges we faced in class. We realized that students had savvy techniques for avoiding work, especially if the work was hard. Recognizing the *why* behind their behaviors helped us see past the action and coach them to do the work. It also helped us avoid falling into an unwinnable trap of reacting to the behavior. After doing this activity ourselves, we decided to share this cast of characters with students. We told them we had met these students over the years and wondered if they recognized any of them. It became a fun way for students to begin to recognize their avoidance behaviors in a nonjudgmental way. We shared our own "characteristics" with our classes too. When I have a difficult task in front of me, for example, I become:

Online Shopper Olivia—So many cute items to put in my cart

When students know that we, too, have defense mechanisms when work gets hard, students are much more open to reflecting and thinking about how to fix it. I also share strategies for refocusing when these characters start to take over. For example, when Online Shopper Olivia wants to tempt me from my work, I negotiate. "OK, Olivia, if I can efficiently focus on this task for the next forty-five minutes, I will take a short break to see what great outfit you want me to put in my cart." (Side note: I rarely actually purchase what is in my cart!)

Casting characters does not mean we excuse or accept unacceptable behaviors in class. There are times when a behavior is disrespectful or harmful, and you

continued →

need to act on it immediately. But in most cases, the behaviors are procrastination and avoidance techniques, and you can much more easily coach or redirect. You can use your professional judgment and understanding of the student to determine if this redirect needs to be one on one and private or used in the moment. Here is an example of how I might redirect a student.

Charlie Charmer: "Thanks, Charlie, for the compliment. I would love to hear more about what you think about my fashion choices after class. Now use that charm of yours to write what you are thinking about Jason Reynold's (2017) book, *Long Way Down*."

Over time, I was able to simply notice the strategies my students were using and name how they were using them to refocus. It was affirming for students not only to independently apply these strategies but also for me to take notice. Sometimes classmates noticed as well.

While students are reading independently, consider using a class engagement chart on a clipboard, like the one shown in figure 1.2. (See page 36 for a blank reproducible version of this figure.)

As students are reading, walk around the room and write down the title of the book or magazine the learner is reading and the number of the page they are on. Record your perception of each student's engagement in the reading zone based on the five-point scale on the chart. You may want to create the scale descriptors for each scale score with your class. Involve them in defining what a 5 looks like, sounds like, and feels like. Conversely, what might a 1 look like, sound like, and feel like? What is in between?

After a few days of collecting this data, you will have enough information to have a coaching conversation with students. During these conversations, you will learn what students like to read and what they don't, when and where they were in their best zone, and what is tripping them up as they read.

Before students can be expected to read independently for twenty minutes per day, they first need to be excited about all the choices they have available to them. As their teacher and literacy leader, you need to model this enthusiasm and be intentional about how to let students know what is available.

Class Engagement Chart

General Behaviors:

- Maintains focus in the reading zone
- Has a book of choice or seeks a recommendation
- Comfortable and awake
- Independently redirects when distracted

Reading Zone Scale:

5—Student's text is in hand and student is focused on the book. Pages are turning, and the student can speak in detail about what they have read.

4—Student is in the zone, has been reading for several minutes straight, and isn't distracted by much of anything. Student can share thoughts and reactions about the book.

3—Student is getting into the zone, reading, but at times distracted. Text is in hand. Sometimes if there is a noise, the student stops reading to attend to the distraction, but can quickly get back into the text. Student can share some thoughts about what they are reading.

2—Student's text is in hand, but the student is sometimes looking around the room and has a difficult time sharing thoughts and reactions to what they read.

1—Student's text is not in hand. Student is doing other things besides reading.

Learning Targets:

- I can sustain a reading zone for a minimum of twenty minutes daily.
- I can understand and manage my own distractions.
- I can self-select "just right" reading material.

Week: 1

For each student, record the book title, page number, and perceived rating scale score (1–5).

Figure 1.2: Class engagement chart example.

continued →

Class Engagement Chart

Student Name	Monday		Tuesday		Wednesday		Thursday		Friday	
	Book, Page	Score	Book, Page	Score	Book, Page	Score	Book, Page	Score	Book, Page	Score
Maria	*Wilder Girls* by Rory Power, p. 27	4	*Wilder Girls*, p. 51	4	*Wilder Girls*, p. 101	5	Absent	N/A	*Debating Darcy* by Sayantani DasGupta, p. 3 (finished *Wilder Girls* while absent)	4
Jerome	*Playing the Cards You're Dealt* by Varian Johnson, p. 56	5	*People* magazine (book at home)	3	*Playing the Cards You're Dealt*, p. 61	3	*People* magazine (book at home)	4	*Playing the Cards You're Dealt*, p. 66	4
Cole	*Punching Bag* by Rex Ogle, p. 7	3	*Punching Bag*, p. 12	4	*Punching Bag*, p. 30	4	Informal reading assessment with instructor	N/A	*Punching Bag*, p. 37	2
Abdullahi	*Black Boy Joy* by Kwame Mbalia, p. 91	4	Small-group with instructor	N/A	*Black Boy Joy*, p. 110	4	*Black Boy Joy*, p. 131	4	*Black Boy Joy*, p. 175	4

Involving Students in Building the Classroom Library

Involving students in the setup of the classroom library can yield many benefits, as listed here. Perhaps most significant, when students get to look through the books, pick them up, look at and read the covers, examine reviews, and page through the text, they begin to see all the types of books available to them. When students discover different genres, authors, and types of books, they are more likely to get excited about reading (Salem, 2018).

1. When students decide how to organize the classroom library, they get an authentic introduction to the books surrounding them. Many adolescent readers aren't aware that some authors write in verse; some write in pictures in the form of graphic novels, or manga; and some use large print, which can be helpful for reluctant readers. The act of browsing through books and deciding which shelves or baskets they should be in serves as a motivator to read and take care of the collection.

2. Students will debate topics and genres as they decide how to organize the library. One student may want all sports books together, while another may be interested in pulling out any sports books that have themes of mystery or romance and putting them in those categories. The discussion raises awareness of the books, their authors, topics, and genres.

3. You will have an opportunity to observe and gather valuable formative assessment data on what students already know and understand about books. You may learn that students want the library organized by topic or genre. Or they may prefer to organize by series. Perhaps they are interested in alphabetizing by author. Some may even want to organize it by color. Don't panic if they choose a way to organize that isn't helpful in finding a good book. Students learn quickly what works and doesn't work for finding books efficiently and effectively. This provides opportunities to make improvements while also creating conditions for authentic learning about organization, books, and the purposes of libraries.

4. Students will build community. Healthy debate, compromise, creativity, and laughter can be expected as students organize the classroom library. Throughout the process, they will get to know one another and begin to create their own unique community of readers.

When students get to tackle the problem of empty walls, you may learn that what *you* find inspirational to hang on them, students may not. A poster saying *Nothing is impossible. The word itself says "I'm Possible"* might incite eye rolls. You might learn that students can feel insulted when surrounded by commercial posters. Or you may experience the opposite. Students might love what you have available to decorate and will revel in choosing where and how it all will come together. Whatever happens, you will get to know students' likes and dislikes. Students will get to negotiate varying tastes. If you have several classes visiting the room throughout the day, learners will know that the community they created is a shared one, so compromises will be necessary.

Be sure to leave several square feet of wall *empty* so that throughout the year, student work can take turns donning the walls in your room. Another important benefit emerging from not littering the classroom walls with commercial posters is there is more room for anchor charts and other instructional materials for students to use.

STORIES FROM THE FIELD

It is late August, and we are starting to gear up for another school year. This particular year, I had the opportunity to teach part time and consult part time. Having been in education for fifteen years, I should have anticipated that the requests for literacy professional learning would come at the start of the year. It also happened to be the summer I had to pack up my entire classroom library and put it in storage because my classroom was getting new carpet.

So, when it came time to have my room ready for the open house, the week prior to school starting, it wasn't done. I remember thinking, "That's OK, I'll go in on Labor Day and at least have my library unpacked and room decorated for the first day of school." When I wasn't able to get in to work on Labor Day, I decided that I would have my students unpack the boxes and put my library together. I felt guilty about this. I didn't think students would be too excited to come in the first day and get to work, especially doing manual labor.

To my surprise, I was so wrong. Students loved unpacking the boxes, looking at each book, deciding how to organize the library, and telling me that all my inspirational posters were cheesy and should definitely not hang them up. They came up with many fun ways to organize the books, including *Go Ahead, Judge a Book by Its Cover* and *Love and War*. The girls thought if they paired romance with war stories that maybe boys and girls might browse together. As students were busy working, I went through and pulled all the favorites from my last cohort of students and put them in a browsing basket titled *Former Student Favs*.

Our classroom library also had several high-interest/low reading level (hi/lo) books from Orca Publishing. These books all had colorful spines. One student enjoyed hunting for them all, putting them on a shelf and dubbing them our "Skittles®" books. I liked this because they were like candy for students. These books are written at a much lower reading level but have high school–relatable topics. I wanted students to devour several of them to build confidence and stamina; but after reading a few, I could recommend books on a similar topic written at a slightly higher reading level.

I learned that honoring student voice in the classroom begins with the environment. And as a bonus, I had a valid reason for not having to spend time decorating my classroom for open house, allowing me a little more time to savor the last moments of summer break.

Honoring Student Voice

In my experience, it's vital for each student to know their value. You want them to understand they are part of a community of learners, and all members of the community need to be invested. One way to create the conditions for this is by making sure to honor students' voices, authentically letting students know that what they have to say matters and won't be judged.

Sometimes, unintentionally, educators can hinder student voice in the classroom by the way they set up desks. If desks are in rows, you send the message that only the voice of the person, usually the teacher, at the front of the room carries value and that any voice heard from the desks will be in response to that lead voice. If instead, you have an environment that lends itself to community time (a place to circle up), group work (desks grouped for collaboration), and independent learning (comfy choice seating throughout the space), you show that you value all the individuals whose contributions make up that community.

Inquiry-based learning naturally invites student voices because it offers opportunities for choice in what students will read and how they will map their journey through the exploration of the topic. Opening up about how students share their learning also lends itself to students shining through their strengths. A few ways to empower students to use their voice (which can be written or verbal) include the following.

- Give students a chance to rehearse what they might share aloud with the class by first writing it down or sharing with a partner.

- Use exit cards, a strategy where students write an idea on a note card, Google form, or sticky note at the end of class, serving as their ticket out of class for the day. Exit cards ensured I heard from every student that day. Exit card questions can be as simple as "What has you stuck?" Or "Where did you experience a breakthrough or discovery today?"

- Give students choices in how they respond to what they are reading rather than a strict set of questions that are the same for everyone. A favorite reader response tool is an I wonder/I notice chart. In one column, students write what they are wondering—their questions—and in the other column, they write their noticings—their observations. The open-ended nature of the assignment, while still somewhat structured, allows students to put their thinking on paper.

Student voice also includes trusting students to make choices for themselves in what they want to read. One way to support that is by using student reading logs.

STORIES FROM THE FIELD

I used to ask students to create a trailer for a favorite book. We would deconstruct several examples of book trailers to create a rubric for elements of an effective video. This was a successful project, but I found that many of the trailers began to look the same. I wondered if we developed a list of criteria for an effective book marketing campaign—would I see more of my students' talents?

Together, we came up with a common rubric, but students could choose their medium. Some chose to create a commercial (or book trailer), some chose a podcast interview with the author, and others created a website. Some students also created posters that we ended up displaying in our school. Ultimately, students were more engaged, and I definitely had more fun evaluating the projects since there was a greater variety.

Student Reading Wish Lists

Having students keep a Someday Reads! log in their notebooks gives them both a place to record books that sound interesting and a launching pad for when they finish a book. Figure 1.3 shows an example Someday Reads! log. (See page 38 for a blank reproducible version of this figure.)

Book Title	Author	Genre	Recommended by	My Rating (when finished reading)
Black Boy Joy	Kwame Mbalia	Story collection Own voices	Abdi	
Wilder Girls	Rory Power	Dystopia	Mrs. Johnson	5 stars!
Every Day	David Levithan	Fantasy/graphic novel	Molly	

Source: Plucker, 2022c.

Figure 1.3: Someday Reads! log example.

Ideas for these books can come from listening to book talks in class, book displays in the school library, student conversations, and independent browsing on sites like Amazon, Barnes and Noble, and Goodreads. Create a collaborative document for student recommendations for books for the classroom library. Students can research the newest award-winning books and add them to the list.

From that list, you can add to your classroom library. Students love this because they feel ownership for the books being added. There are several resources you can use to obtain money to fund your classroom library. Community organizations, such as your local American Legion, Rotary Club, or Lions Club often have funds available, and they are waiting to be asked. Consider ordering books around winter break so the boxes arrive early in the new calendar year. Students can then open the boxes (which feel like presents to them) and negotiate with one another who gets which book first.

Legacy Books

At the end of the year, ask students to choose a book from the classroom library that has had a lasting impact on them. For whatever reason, the student kept thinking about the characters and story long after they finished the book and moved on to another. Ask them to write a sentence or two on how the book impacted them inside the front cover. They can sign their name and add their graduation year. You might find students stopping back into your room to see if any other students have added notes to their legacy books.

You might consider printing stickers for students to record their legacy thoughts to place inside their books. Figure 1.4 shows an example legacy book label. (See page 39 for a blank reproducible version of this figure.)

Legacy Book
Book title: Crackback by John Coy
You are going to **love** this book because: It is an action-packed book filled with Miles making questionable decisions because he wants to win football games so bad! You won't be able to put this down.
Signed,
Name: Jack Thomas
Graduation year: 2019

Figure 1.4: Legacy book label.

End-of-Year Reflection Videos

At the end of the year, have students create a video previewing what new students will experience in your class. This video serves two purposes: (1) it reflects the fun and growth that students experienced, and (2) it previews for new students what they can expect in the course. Let students pick groups to work in and brainstorm as a class all that has been accomplished during the year. Gather photos and other artifacts from your time together. Give students time to write their storyboard, collect their video clips, edit, polish, and publish. Consider sharing the videos with other classes and providing awards for most creative, most convincing, best in show, and others.

Reader-Response Journals

Reader-response journals don't need to be fancy or complicated. Simply ask students to bring in a composition notebook and tape a list of prompts at the front, as shown in figure 1.5. Students only need to use these prompts if they have a hard time getting started.

Tapping Prior Knowledge
• I already know that . . .   • This reminds me of . . .   • This relates to . . .
Asking Questions
• I wonder why . . .   • What if . . .   • How come . . .
Predicting
• I'll bet that . . .   • I think . . .   • If _____, then . . .
Visualizing
• I can picture . . .   • In my mind I see . . .   • If this were a movie . . .
Making Connections
• This reminds me of . . .   • I experienced this once when . . .   • I can relate to this because . . .
Adopting an Alignment
• The character I most identify with is . . .   • I really got into this story when . . .   • I can relate to this author because . . .
Forming Interpretations
• What this means to me is . . .   • I think this represents . . .   • The idea I'm getting is . . .
Monitoring
• I got lost here because . . .   • I need to reread the part where . . .   • I know I'm on the right track because . . .

Source: Adapted from Olson & Land, 2007.

Figure 1.5: Reader-response journal prompts.

continued →

Revising Meaning
• At first, I thought _____, but now . . .   • My latest thought about this is . . .   • I'm getting a different picture here because . . .
Analyzing the Author's Craft
• A memorable line for me is . . .   • This word or phrase stands out for me because . . .   • I like how the author uses _____ to show . . .
Reflecting and Reacting
• So, the big idea is . . .   • A conclusion I'm drawing is . . .   • This is relevant to my life because . . .
Evaluating
• I [like/don't like] _____ because . . .   • This could be more effective if . . .   • The most important message is . .

Visit **go.SolutionTree.com/literacy** for a free reproducible version of this figure.

After being in the reading zone for twenty minutes, ask students to respond to what they read for five minutes. Be transparent with students that this isn't completely authentic. We don't usually carry notebooks when we go to the beach or coffee shop to read for pleasure, and reading for enjoyment is the goal during zone reading. Explain that we sometimes put our thoughts on Amazon reviews or Goodreads, and take notes of what we want to discuss with others reading the book or during our book club meeting. The reader-response journal is an opportunity for students to share their thinking, and it can give you a window into their comprehension strengths and areas of need. You can use these journals to prompt students to think deeper or differently. It can serve as a critical tool for conferring as well.

Critique

When students have permission to voice their likes and dislikes about a text, they will be able to utilize text evidence and logical reasoning more quickly. You can discover adolescents' aptitude for critique when asking questions such as, "Are there characters in the book that you think are not believable? Why?" "Where do you think the author gets off track?" "If you could give this author advice for further improvements, what would you say?" You may find that students are hesitant at first to criticize a published piece of writing, but when assured it is not only OK, but that authors expect it, students will unleash their opinions.

Creating Scarcity for the Hottest Reads

To make the most of a classroom library budget and strive for the greatest variety and diversity in your book collection, consider not having any duplicates of books at first. This means that there will only be one copy of the book that is the most popular, or the *hottest read*. You can certainly encourage students to check the school and local libraries for books they want to read that are currently checked out, but you may find that students will engage with their peers to hurry them along, if necessary. It may also raise the level of concern for some readers to find time to read outside of class if they know a line is forming for the book they want. Often those lines form because of something a student shares in class about the book. This elevated student agency and intrinsic motivation encourages students to finish so their peers can read it, and they can eventually talk about it.

In a study by Gay Ivey and Peter H. Johnston (2013), in which students had experienced similar scarcity, the authors found additional benefits:

> Social agency was readily observable in the classrooms. For instance, we witnessed Dean persuading Gavin: "You really should read *Wish You Were Dead*. It's by Todd Strasser, who wrote *Give a Boy a Gun*, and you got me to read that." (p. 263)

The authors go on to discuss how students interacted with each other in authentic, yet surprising ways outside the classroom (Ivey & Johnston, 2013). Students who didn't typically hang out together were now eating lunch at the same table in order to talk about a book they had in common, for example.

Another benefit of not stocking up on several copies of a specific title is that from year to year, cohort to cohort, the hottest reads will change. Encouraging students to wait their turn for the hottest book to read creates anticipation and intrinsic motivation for reading.

Offering Authentic Literacy Activities

Authentic literacy involves providing various opportunities for students to read and write for a distinct purpose (Duke, Purcell-Gates, Hall, & Tower, 2006; Schmoker, 2011). Neil K. Duke and colleagues (2006) define *authentic literacy* as "activities in the classroom that replicate or reflect reading and writing activities that occur in the lives of people outside of a learning-to-read-and-write context and purpose" (p. 346).

When you give students an authentic purpose for reading, writing, and problem solving, you can engage them further.

Giving students opportunities to contribute to their community in authentic ways can, in turn, build community in the classroom. You might have students perform a readers' theater for elementary students, read to preschoolers, or interview local seniors at a nearby independent living senior apartment building about historical moments in their lives. These activities provide authentic opportunities to engage in literacy.

STORIES FROM THE FIELD

When I first started teaching the ninth-grade reading intervention class, I wanted to be sure students felt comfortable, so when they asked if I was going to make them read out loud, I was quick to respond, "Not if you don't want to." But then I heard many of them read to me during conferencing and knew we needed to work on fluency. However, I couldn't jump right into readers' theater because I had told them I wouldn't make them read aloud in front of their peers. So, I had to think creatively.

Our library had just received a grant for headphones for students to use in creating podcasts. I figured students would think it was novel to use the new equipment, so I had them each grab a children's book they hadn't read before, and we headed to the lab to record. Not one student objected to doing a cold read, recording it for later listening.

We spent a week playing games that helped students consider punctuation, phrasing, volume, pausing, rate, and more, while they read. They thought about how their choices impacted their understanding of the text. Because these were games, students were more apt to participate. I did hold true to my promise of not making anyone read aloud if they didn't want to. Fortunately, students weren't objecting.

After a week of fluency activities and practice, I asked students to revisit the children's book they had recorded earlier in the week. They went through the text, considering how to say each line in order to deliver it in the way they felt the author wanted readers to hear and understand it. After a day of practice, we headed back to the media center to record new versions of the story. I asked students to listen to both recordings and write a reflection on the changes made. This helped cement the need to consider fluency when reading, whether aloud or silently.

To my surprise, after this activity, many students asked to do more performing. We moved into readers' theater and, upon students' request, scheduled a trip to the elementary school down the street so students could perform their stories (in groups) for first graders. This got students excited, and they worked harder knowing they would have an audience.

Exploring Community Engagement Opportunities

Look around your school community. Are there opportunities for students to engage with others in the community without having to arrange busing and funding for a complicated field trip? Does your school have a preschool program in which students could read to the children? Is there an elementary school within walking distance where your students could perform some readers' theater or develop book buddies? Is there a senior housing complex nearby? Students could hear true stories of how reading and writing impact these older members of their community. In turn, residents could ask students about their reading and writing lives, helping them understand the value of not only reading and writing, but also of sharing that part of themselves with others.

Building a community of readers, writers, communicators, and thinkers can have a profound impact on students' belief in their ability to achieve results. When you believe you can achieve, it increases motivation (Zheng, 2022). Learning is hard, but when students enter a classroom environment that is positive, welcoming, warm, and inclusive, they are much more likely to embrace the challenge and remember the feeling of belonging long after class is over (Luther, 2022).

You may connect students to larger communities as well. In 2010, Pernille Ripp launched The Global Read Aloud (n.d.). According to the website:

The premise is simple; we pick a book to read aloud to our students during a set 6-week period and during that time we try to make as many global connections as possible. Each teacher decides how much time they would like to dedicate and how involved they would like to be. . . . Teachers get a community of other educators to do a global project with, hopefully inspiring them to continue these connections through the year. (The Global Read Aloud, n.d.)

This endeavor provides opportunities for educators and students to connect with others experiencing the same story across the globe. World Read Aloud Day, One Book, One School/City are other community-wide events that can help students make connections with their reading to others outside the small circle of your classroom community.

Getting Started

Consider the following ideas for developing authentic and lasting relationships with students and building your community of readers, writers, thinkers, and communicators.

1. **Use any activities you have tried in the past that authentically help you get to know your students:** For example, I worked with a team of ELA teachers who were part of a school system that did home visits. During the visits, the teachers brought a few books from the classroom library and had each student pick one. Maybe you create a trivia game with fun facts about students at the beginning of the year, or you ask parents to fill out an online survey so you can get to know students' reading history and personal lives. These and many more "get-to-know-you" activities are tried and true, and you should keep using them.

2. **Drop activities that aren't effective:** If you have activities from the past that felt forced, didn't engage students in the way you hoped, or that students resisted, feel free to throw them out. I used to do an icebreaker in which students wrote questions on a note card. Then they got up to find a student they didn't know, and asked each other the questions. On the surface, it wasn't a bad activity, but it always felt forced, and students were vocal about feeling awkward. They needed to know each other better first; then they would feel more comfortable asking each other personal questions.

3. **Weave community themes into your first unit of study:** Find ways to connect learning to the goals you have for being a reading, writing, and learning community. Goals for community likely include creating shared beliefs and values, building relationships so collaboration and connection is authentic, and developing an acceptance and tolerance for differences within the group. Weave in texts, writing tasks, and group activities that allow students to practice and work toward achieving those goals.

4. **Bring student voice into the norms you set as a community:** Ask students what kind of community they want to experience and contribute to while learning together. In my class, we created common agreements on chart paper. We added, changed, and deleted ideas until we had a set of norms everyone in the class agreed to. Everyone signed it, and I posted it on the wall. To get the ideas flowing, students reflected on and described the best and worst teams, classes, and communities they had experienced. This helped each student come up with a set of expectations for the individual, the teacher, and the group for how we should act and interact during class.

Conclusion

One of the most powerful motivators for learning is positive emotions. Additionally, the need to experience connection with others through meaningful relationships leads to student agency and intrinsic motivation (Zheng, 2022). As educators, we have a responsibility to take the time and be intentional in fostering a community in our classrooms. This requires getting to know our students as readers, writers, thinkers, and all around young people.

Class Engagement Chart

General Behaviors:

- Maintains focus in the reading zone
- Has a book of choice or seeks a recommendation
- Comfortable and awake
- Independently redirects when distracted

Reading Zone Scale:

5—Student's text is in hand and student is focused on the book. Pages are turning, and the student can speak in detail about what they have read.

4—Student is in the zone, has been reading for several minutes straight, and isn't distracted by much of anything. Student can share thoughts and reactions about the book.

3—Student is getting into the zone, reading, but at times distracted. Text is in hand. Sometimes if there is a noise, the student stops reading to attend to the distraction, but can quickly get back into the text. Student can share some thoughts about what they are reading.

2—Student's text is in hand, but the student is sometimes looking around the room and has a difficult time sharing thoughts and reactions to what they read.

1—Student's text is not in hand. Student is doing other things besides reading.

Learning Targets:

- I can sustain a reading zone for a minimum of twenty minutes daily.
- I can understand and manage my own distractions.
- I can self-select "just right" reading material.
- .
- .
- .

Week: _____

For each student, record book title, page number, and perceived rating scale score (1–5).

Student Name	Monday		Tuesday		Wednesday		Thursday		Friday	
	Book, Page	Score	Book, Page	Score	Book, Page	Score	Book, Page	Score	Book, Page	Score

Inspiring Lifelong Readers © 2024 Solution Tree Press • SolutionTree.com
Visit **go.SolutionTree.com/literacy** to download this free reproducible.

Someday Reads! Log

Book Title	Author	Genre	Recommended by	My Rating (when finished reading)

Source: Plucker, J. M. (2022c). Prioritize helping our students fall in love with reading (again). Accessed at https://mackinlearning.com/prioritize-helping-our-students-fall-in-love-with-reading-again on July 5, 2023.

Legacy Book Template

Legacy Book

Book title: _____

You are going to *love* this book because:

Signed,

Name: _____

Graduation year: _____

Legacy Book

Book title: _____

You are going to *love* this book because:

Signed,

Name: _____

Graduation year: _____

Legacy Book

Book title: _____

You are going to *love* this book because:

Signed,

Name: _____

Graduation year: _____

CHAPTER 2

Immersing Adolescents in Rich, Diverse Text

When I first started teaching the ninth-grade reading intervention class in 2009, I wanted to be sure my room was filled with books students would want to read. I had visions of bookshelves filled with a variety of young adult (YA) books and decorated with browsing baskets, themed displays, and neat section labels. I envied the classroom librarians of my elementary colleagues, but I needed money to be able to purchase books and bookshelves. With this vision in mind, I sat down at my computer to first write a grant.

While I waited to hear if I was going to get any funding, I started searching on websites like Amazon and Barnes and Noble to find the greatest collection of books students would race to my room to check out. In mere seconds, I started to panic. So many choices! So many genres! And then I realized I had absolutely no idea how to build an engaging classroom library for reluctant, resistant, and striving readers. I didn't even know how to build one for ravenous readers. I had been teaching the same canon of novels for several years, and my own reading was consumed with beach reads, memoirs, and historical fiction—my favorites, but likely not what teens would want to read.

So, I visited my friend, a school librarian, and asked for help. While I know the librarian could have created a great list for me, she actually encouraged me to call Mackin, an education company she worked with who had a team of teachers who knew the best and newest tried-and-true titles for my student population. I was quick to tell her I didn't have any money yet, and when I did get some, I didn't want to spend it on hiring someone to build me a list. She reassured me that the service was free.

With relief, I sent off an email to the Mackin Classroom team describing my dilemma, and in a week's time, I had a list of the most beautiful, engaging books, most of which I had never heard of. (Mackin's team of former teachers still provide this free service. You can fill out a resource development form and they will get to work curating a list from their catalog of over 4.2 million print and digital books [Mackin, 2021]). The list included a variety of nonfiction books, fiction books in various genres and forms (graphic novels, novels in verse, large print, illustrated novels, collections of short stories), hi/lo books, and more. As I looked through the list, I noticed the variety of backgrounds, settings, cultures, and experiences the protagonists represented and thought to myself, "I just know my students will be able to see themselves somewhere in this collection of stories." Long story short, the grant money was awarded, book-shelves were purchased, a collection ordered, and my library was ready for readers by the first day of school.

But what will you do with a great classroom library if students aren't motivated to read? This chapter explores various ways you can get students excited about reading, redefines the meaning of *literacy* and *text* for students, and finally, offers ideas for helping students develop a lifelong love of reading. It also discusses how to moti-vate adolescent readers, the complexity of literacy, and the importance and impact of immersing students in rich, diverse texts.

Motivating Adolescent Readers

Motivational supports are necessary for student engagement in reading. Students need to feel competent and confident to reduce perceived difficulty and prevent resis-tance to or avoidance of reading. Following these principles can help students become more motivated to read.

- **Seek mastery:** Students engage in tasks and are motivated to keep going when they are working toward mastering a skill. I employed an "ABC, do it over" policy for all major assessments. This means that if students are not at least proficient (translated to a grade of C) on the rubric for the assessment, they receive an incomplete in the gradebook and additional opportunities to master the literacy skill (Plucker, 2022a).

- **Pursue meaning:** Readers will persist through any text if they are able to make sense of what they are reading. This is why it is so helpful to ask students to record their thinking while they read.

- **Offer choice:** One way to increase student motivation to read is to provide choices. When students receive even just two options, their motivation for completing the task increases.

- **Transfer control:** When students take a passive approach to learning, it may seem easier because you are leading and students are doing what you ask. The reality is that when teachers are in control, students may disengage and learning is stifled (Plucker, 2022a). One way to let go of control is to embrace questioning in the classroom. Each time you feel like giving students an answer, turn it back to them by saying, "What are you thinking? What in the text is making you think that?" "What are you wondering about now?"

- **Make reading a social activity:** Educator Amy Lamatina (2023) advises: "We are social learners! Having a safe space to talk about books and express opinions can help students develop a deeper understanding of their own reading preferences."

When you help students see the value in reading, emphasizing the importance of time spent reading, students' motivation levels increase. Since adolescents are social beings, you can capitalize on that desire by arranging for students to collaborate with one another, which also increases motivation for reading (Guthrie & Klouda, 2014). This means moving desks out of rows and creating groups of desks for natural proximity and group work. You also can intentionally plan for lessons in which students are required to work with one another. When you lean into these motivations—and students feel more confident, can make choices, understand *why* reading is essential and enjoyable, and share learning with peers—you have a greater chance of fostering lifelong readers.

Redefining *Literacy* and *Text*

While a dictionary may define *literacy* simply as the ability to read and write, it is necessary to broaden the definition for students, or you may limit their opportunities to practice the critical literacy skills needed to compete globally. Teachers need to understand the complexity of literacy so they are better able to offer opportunities for students to advance their reading, writing, and speaking skills. According to the United Nations Educational, Scientific, and Cultural Organization (UNESCO; 2017), literacy is:

> The ability to identify, understand, interpret, create, communicate and compute, using printed and written materials associated with varying contexts. Literacy involves a continuum of learning in enabling individuals to achieve their goals, to develop their knowledge and potential, and to participate fully in their community and wider society.

In other words, literacy is thinking. Literacy is learning how to learn. Broadly defining literacy helps to simplify how students are already engaging in literacy activities through their passions. Watching and re-watching the YouTube videos of snowboarder Shawn White so his moves can be emulated on the slopes is literacy. Studying the playbook for Friday's football game is literacy. Learning the vocabulary words *arabesque, cambré,* and *entrechat* allows the dancer to more efficiently respond to the directions of the ballet choreographer, which also is literacy. Not only must you know and understand this, you must be sure that your students do as well.

As with the definition of literacy, you should also redefine *text* for students. When students tackle the complex analysis of visual and digital texts, such as advertisements, satirical cartoons, and video clips, they can affirm the comprehension skills they have already mastered. When you ask students to translate those thinking skills to print, this is one way to build their confidence. Therefore, as educators, we have a responsibility to discover the literacy lives of students in order to bridge the skills they are applying to written text.

To help students see this transfer, I asked them to record their thinking while watching a YouTube tutorial or other how-to video of their choice. Figure 2.1 illustrates this activity. (See page 60 for a blank reproducible version of this figure.)

Cultivating Lifelong Readers

When thinking about the goal of creating lifelong readers, it is important to remind yourself of the revised definitions of *literacy* and *text*. As educators, we want students to understand that being a lifelong reader means being dedicated to reading, learning, thinking, discussing, critiquing, and examining multiple perspectives, as well as reading for pleasure and as an escape. Students can step outside the notion that lifelong readers

Tutorial video title: *How to Make a Notebook in Canva*
Creator: *Rhonda Denise (2021)*
Video URL: *www.youtube.com/watch?v=WUkY9-D5qkw*
I notice . . .
Rhonda tells us why she is making the video.
She isn't afraid to make mistakes and keep going.
I predict . . .
I am going to have to pause several times as I work on my own Canva design.
I predict this will take me a lot longer to create than the ten minutes it took her.
I am confused by . . .
How she is toggling back and forth between two designs
How she copied the logo
I learned. . . or I'm wondering . . .
How to pull the color code and copy it to a new design
The thinking behind the design process
How the journal gets printed; Rhonda shows how to create it and discusses the size of the paper, but then what?
I think the creator wants me to . . .
Rhonda wants me to know that she coaches others in creating designs.
She wants me to know I can take her Canva course for only $25. I might have to do that!

Figure 2.1: Comprehending a tutorial.

are only the individuals who always have a book in hand. For students to see themselves as readers, they need to have positive and enjoyable experiences with books. Educators have a responsibility to match students with books that incite that kind of enjoyment and excitement. Following are eight strategies for helping you cultivate lifelong readers.

1. Flood the environment with books.

2. Ensure the classroom collection is inclusive.

3. Ask students what they want to read.

4. Make time for reading in school.

5. Collaborate with your school librarian.

6. Be your students' coach.

7. Balance print and digital texts.

8. Talk books . . . all the time.

Flood the Environment With Books

In order to find that one significant book, the one that students who haven't had positive experiences with books get lost in, the one for which students come bounding up to you and say, "I finished. I didn't want it to end! Now what do I read?" you must surround students with lots of books. In Kelly Gallagher's (2009) *Readicide*, Gallagher states, "Let me be clear: if we are to have any chance of developing a reading habit in our students, they must be immersed in a K–12 'book flood'—a term coined by researcher Warwick Elley (1991)" (p. 43).

This book flood provides a tsunami of choice, making it nearly impossible for a student to say, "I don't have anything to read." As author and educator Debbie Miller (2008) writes, "When children are surrounded by books, we're showing them that reading is important throughout the day; reading is infused into almost everything we do" (p. 34). Students' home libraries have a direct impact on their literacy as well. According to a study completed at the University of Nevada, Reno (2010):

> Being raised in a bookless home compared to being raised in a home
> with a 500-book library has as great an effect on the level of education
> a child will attain as having parents who are barely literate (3 years of
> education) compared to having parents who have a university education
> (15 or 16 years of education).

As much as you may be aware of this, it can be difficult to control how many books students have at home. This is why it is imperative that you send books home with students and not allow the fear of not getting them back to hinder that practice. Ebooks are a great option if students have access to a suitable digital device and you want them reading the same book both at home and in the classroom. Most ebooks are available for offline reading on a device and make it nearly impossible for students to say, "I left my book at home," since they almost always have their device with them. You might encourage some students to have a book in the classroom and a separate book at home. Students, even striving readers, can have more than one book going at one time.

STORIES FROM THE FIELD

By the time we start nearing breaks (my school has a fall break in October, another for Thanksgiving, and then a long break for winter), my colleagues and I start gearing up to send books home with students. We want them to have several—for choice, for when they finish one and will need to begin another, or for when they need to abandon a book. Leading up to the first break, we spend time brainstorming how students can "steal" minutes for reading during the day.

I find that students enjoy brainstorming ways to sneak in extra time. They say things like, "While I am waiting for my mom to pick me up after school" or "If I am reading before supper, sometimes I won't be interrupted to do my chore of setting the table." One student facetiously suggests putting the book in a large plastic zipper bag and reading while showering. A few days before break, we spend time making a list of books to have at home and a plan for when we will dedicate time to read. Students all write specifically about how they will try to steal extra minutes. When students return from break, we reflect. During fall break, it seems fewer students are meeting their goal, but by the return from winter break, most students have developed a habit of reading at home.

As summer approached, my colleagues and I were worried about how reading habits would last over the summer for our first year of academic literacy students. So, we developed a plan to send students home with a stack of books. Of course, we were nervous. What if we didn't get them back? What if the books stayed in students' backpacks all summer long? We decided we would host a Books and BBQ gathering midsummer as a time to come back together as a community and for an opportunity to swap out read or abandoned books with a new set. This would give us a reason to send fewer books home and risk fewer not returned.

To our surprise, more than half our students attended the Books and BBQ event *and* brought books to exchange. We enjoyed the community, a little kickball, some good old-fashioned hotdogs, chips, and soda, and authentic conversation about books. And if you are wondering if we got our books back the following fall—mostly, yes. However, we did bribe students to get them. We visited sophomore English classes and asked students to check their rooms, under their beds, in their backpacks, and in their cars, and to return any books with

continued →

our school's name stamped on it. We got so many books and more. We ended up taking back public library books and returning books to students' middle schools. What did it cost us? A lollipop per book. Worth it!

Ensure the Classroom Collection Is Inclusive

As you build your classroom library, it is essential to offer a diverse book collection for students. All students deserve to see themselves in books. Students from majority groups experience this frequently, sometimes without even noticing it. But when students do not feel like they can find books that represent their stories, they definitely notice.

Inclusive classroom libraries include a variety of stories with characters of varying race, ethnicity, culture, social class, LGBTQ identities, neurological and physical differences, citizenship status, religions, and other social statuses. When individuals can see their stories positively in books, it helps them to develop positive self-identities (Braga, 2022). Diverse characters also provide new perspectives for young people to learn about other groups in a positive way. This is why "own voices" texts are recognized as so valuable. These are stories told by authors who come from the cultures and have the experiences they are writing about versus books written by people without those lived experiences.

When searching for books to add to your inclusive classroom library, look to School Library Journal and Scholastic 2020 School Librarian of the Year, Cicely Lewis, who started a movement to inspire more inclusive reading practices. She and her followers have amazing recommendations. Following the hashtags #ownvoices and #weneeddiversebooks also provides helpful direction in creating inclusive collections.

As you examine texts, be careful that you are not choosing books that perpetuate stereotypes. Ask yourself, "Does this hi/lo book perpetuate a potentially dangerous narrative that students striving to read also struggle with drugs or get involved with gangs?" Be intentional in vetting books for your collection. Ask questions such as, "Are all types of people represented?" "Am I making sure that all the books about people of color are not just historical?" "Do I have books about Indigenous people living in the present?" If a book features a marginalized group, is it also focused on trauma? Certainly, historical books and books with characters overcoming trauma can be extremely valuable. But do you also include books in which students get to read about young people of all kinds with normal, everyday childhood experiences?

The goal is not only to have positive representations but to have a variety of representations, particularly those that express joy. As my colleague and sociologist, Kia Heise said, "Majority groups get to be represented in all their wonderful and flawed humanity and minority groups deserve the same" (K. Heise, personal communication, September 14, 2020).

Ask Students What They Want to Read

When you include students in refreshing the classroom library, they feel like it is theirs. If possible, reserve some funds for adding to your library throughout the year. Students can keep a running wish list. Parents and parent organizations are often looking to spend money in a way that supports students; and when literacy is the goal, the funding is often approved. One strategy is to seek out students' requested books from the school library or public library and bring them (on loan) to the classroom. Eventually, students will want to take their own field trip to their school media center or local library, but until then, don't be afraid to bring the requests to students. They will feel special because you intentionally took the time to find that requested book just for them.

Students can be involved in a myriad of ways that do not require additional purchases. For example, students can set up displays of their favorite reads. They can write short reviews that hang from the shelf next to the book like you might see at a bookstore. When students' opinions about books are valued, students' identities as readers grow.

Make Time for Reading in School

We know that to become a better reader, one needs to read. Unfortunately, the time students receive for reading during the school day diminishes as they get older. Independent reading programs, like silent sustained reading (SSR) and drop everything and read (DEAR), get mixed results on their effectiveness in promoting student growth in literacy (Regional Educational Laboratory Program, 2017). This is partly due to how the programs are implemented (Willingham, 2015). Simply providing time without content-rich and conversation-rich environments may not result in students actually reading during the dedicated time. Regardless, Daniel Willingham (2015) states, "If we really want students to be leisure readers, we must find ways to inspire a desire to read in students who do not get such inspiration at home." Students who read just fifteen minutes more each day will see accelerated literacy growth (Renaissance, 2016).

In a fifty-minute class period, my colleagues and I would hold sacred twenty minutes for students to read. After students spent twenty minutes in their zone, ideally at a 1–5 rating scale score of 4 or 5 on the class engagement chart (see figure 1.2, page 21), we would have them write for five minutes using the reader-response journal prompts (see figure 1.5, page 29). Sometimes students would be ready to think more critically, or the book they were reading would call for critical thinking. When this was necessary, we would have students choose from critical-reading prompts (see figure 2.2), which we would have them attach to the back of their reader-response journals.

Author's Purpose or Message

- The author's purpose for writing is . . .
- The reason the author wrote this passage is . . .
- The author is writing this section to . . .
- The big idea in the writing is . . .
- The author is showing me that _____ because . . .
- The author's message is . . .

Point of View

- When I read _____, I can see the author feels . . .
- The author feels that _____, because . . .
- This passage suggests that the author's opinion about . . .
- The author is clearly suggesting . . .

Tone or Bias

- The tone of this passage seems to be _____ because . . .
- The author's feelings about _____ can best be described as . . .
- I notice the author uses the word or phrase _____, which makes me think they feel . . .
- It is clear that the author wants . . .
- The writer is taking the stance that . . .
- This writer believes that . . .
- I know the writer feels _____, because they . . .

Power or Motivation

- The character holding the power in this section is . . .
- If the power shifted, I believe _____ could happen.
- The character uses their power to . . .

Author Credibility

- The author provides support by . . .
- The author is best qualified to say . . .
- The writer is making the assumption that . . .
- The author used _____ to support their ideas about . . .

Author Craft
• Writers of nonfiction help readers by . . .
• When the writer _____, it helps make a strong point because . . .
• When the writer uses words like . . .
• Authors use . . .
• Writers always . . .
• This is powerful because the author . . .
• I notice that authors or writers will _____, which helps me because . . .
General Critical Thinking
• When I see _____, it makes me think . . .
• When the author did _____, I thought . . .
• The writer says _____, but I think . . .
• I will use this information to . . .
• This information seems . . .
• The writer's opinion about _____ is . . .
Perspective
• I can describe this character's perspective as . . .
• The other side would say . . .
• To play devil's advocate, I would tell the character to . . .
• My advice to the character is to . . .

Figure 2.2: Critical-reading prompts.

*Visit **go.SolutionTree.com/literacy** for a free reproducible version of this figure.*

Readers' responses to these prompts can be valuable tools for assessment and coaching. When reading these responses, we can see student thinking, which can be helpful in identifying areas with which they might need support with comprehension. This tool is especially helpful in planning for guided reading groups and one-on-one conferences with readers.

Collaborate With Your School Librarian

The library is the heart of the school, and the media specialist can serve as everyone's teacher. Deb Svec, the librarian at Palm Beach Gardens High School in Florida, runs a program in which students volunteer to eat their lunches in the library and talk about books. She calls it "Lit at Lunch" (2020). It is inspiring how she is able to bring together students who don't necessarily run in the same social circles and get them excited about books and conversation. The librarian can, and usually wants to, partner with teachers to engage and advance readers. As experts in current titles, curation of resources on timely topics, and research techniques to rival Google, they are invaluable to the pursuit of literacy growth.

Be Your Students' Coach

Often, in the pursuit to use every minute of class time to its fullest, educators can fall into managing student behavior instead of engaging and inviting them into the process of owning their learning. A quick search of Merriam-Webster's (n.d.b) definitions for *manage* includes "to handle or direct" and "to make and keep compliant." Adolescents do not want to be handled or directed. They definitely don't want anyone to force them to be compliant. Do you? Educators can sometimes find themselves falling into managing student behaviors with quick commands like, "Please put your makeup away; it's our reading time" or "Do you really have to go to the nurse right now?" It is easy to end up in a whack-a-mole game with students, and nobody will win. If you instead switch to *engaging* students, which Merriam-Webster (n.d.a) defines as "to give attention to, to induce to participate, or to bring together," students will work with you, not against you.

One way to shift from managing students to engaging them is to focus on being their coach. On the field or in a music room, students get better at their craft when instructors coach them in small and incremental improvements. In a voice lesson, a teacher might ask the student to sing a few measures. The voice teacher listens first. At some point, the teacher might ask the singer to stop and reflect, receive some instruction, and possibly hear some modeling before singing those measures again. Similarly, on the soccer field, athletes practice a play, and the coach watches various players, sometimes just one, intently. The coach studies the playbook and reflects on the decisions made. The coach blows a whistle and gives discrete instruction for small changes that need to be made. The athletes listen, reflect, and when the coach blows the whistle again, they try again. Both the singer and athlete may need several opportunities to get it just right.

The instruction, encouragement, and opportunities to try and fail as many times as possible before game day or a recital are what engage and motivate learners. This ultimately leads to better performances as well. We need to be our students' coach in the classroom as they strive to become better readers, writers, and communicators. A helpful tool to accomplish this by using the class-engagement chart (see figure 1.2, page 21). When kept conveniently on an iPad or clipboard, this chart provides an easy access point for recording data to use later in a coaching situation.

STORIES FROM THE FIELD

It's early in the school year, and we are working hard to hold sacred twenty minutes of independent reading every day. We know that this is one of the primary strategies we must use to advance the literacy skills for each student in the class. I am collecting data on the class engagement chart during zone reading time. I am interested in the book each student is reading, the page number they are on when I come around to check, and a perception of how "in the zone" they are based on a rating scale we developed together—5 meaning they are locked in, and 1 meaning they are not really reading and very easily distracted or perhaps distracting to others.

Today is Wednesday, and I am most concerned about Carlos. He has been reading a book called *Black Boy White School* by Brian F. Walker (2012). According to my data (see figure 2.3, page 54), Carlos has been consistently reading the book all week and seems to be progressing through from page 6 to 114, but my perception of his ability to stay in his zone is low: 1s and 2s. It's time for a conference.

During the conference, I learn that Carlos is reading his book. He can tell me all about Anthony "Ant" and his decision to leave his East Cleveland school and attend Belton Academy on scholarship. Carlos has a lot to say about the interactions Ant encounters in a "rich White school." So, I ask Carlos if he is enjoying the book and when he is finding time to read. He assures me that he really likes the book and that he reads during study hall later in the day when he isn't so tired. We come up with a plan together for him to still get his reading time in during our class as well. Carlos chooses to bring a snack to class on Thursday and see if it helps him stay awake.

From the data in figure 2.3, it seems to have helped. He was in his reading zone at a rating scale score of 4. Choosing to coach Carlos not only improved his reading zone, but also our relationship, especially since I didn't penalize him for struggling to maintain his reading stamina earlier in the week.

Week: 1
For each student, record the book title, page number, and rating scale score (1-5).

Student Name	Monday		Tuesday		Wednesday		Thursday		Friday		Notes
Carlos	*Black Boy White School* by Brian Walker (2012), p. 6	1	*Black Boy White School*, p. 67	2	*Black Boy White School*, p. 114	2	*Black Boy White School*, p. 141	4	*Black Boy White School*, p. 175	4	
Tyler	*People magazine*	3	*Scholastic Book of World Records* by Jenifer Corr Morse (2011)	3	*People magazine*	3	*Crackback* by John Coy (2010), p 10	4	*Crackback*, p. 19	5	
Aimee	*Cirque du Freak #1* by Darren Shan (2002), p. 8	4	*Cirque du Freak #1,* p. 28	4	*Cirque du Freak #1,* p. 47	4	*Cirque du Freak #1,* p. 63	4	*Absent*		
Brandi	*Ana's Story* by Jenna Bush (2007), p. 12	4	*Ana's Story,* p. 28	4	*Ana's Story,* p. 96	4	*Ana's Story,* p. 121	5	*Ana's Story,* p. 140	5	
Mohammed	*Juice* by Eric Walters (2005), p. 10	4			*Juice,* p. 40		*Juice,* p. 51	4	*Juice,* p. 61	4	
Kiera	*The Notebook* by Nicholas Spark (2014), p. 7	4	*The Notebook,* p. 20	4	*The Notebook,* p. 40	4	*People magazine*	4	*The Notebook,* p. 50	4	
Alissa	*Twilight* by Stephenie Meyer (2005), p. 7	4	*Twilight,* p. 21	4	*Twilight,* p. 41	4	*Twilight,* p. 71	4	*Twilight,* p. 90	4	

Mohammed, Kiera, and Alissa together . . . distracting!

Figure 2.3: Class-engagement chart example.

Balance Print and Digital Texts

In her book, *Reader, Come Home,* Maryanne Wolf (2018) cautions that because engagement with digital texts have altered people's reading brains in a way that may be causing a decline in learners' critical thinking, teachers should keep print texts a priority for developing readers. Wolf goes on to warn that digital reading may be negatively affecting deep engagement with text and people's ability to show empathy. When people engage in digital texts, they tend to skim, read in short bursts, and seek to synthesize an overload of information. The reality is, digital reading is prominent in our culture, so teachers need to help students find balance.

Ebooks; audiobooks; digital texts with professional narration, sometimes referred to as read-alongs; text-to-speech options; and interactive texts can be important tools for engaging readers. Most ebook digital platforms provide students with tools to enhance their reading experience. Readers can personalize their experience by switching the page spread from two to one, customize the background and font color, enlarge the text, use text-to-speech or narration features, and change the font.

These choices allow students to create the digital environment that is most comfortable for them, much like they choose a comfortable physical environment to settle into a good book. Many ebooks also provide tools for interacting with the text, such as highlighting, note-taking, bookmarks, embedded dictionaries, and opportunities to organize and export notes for use later. Educators have a responsibility to familiarize students with these tools and create opportunities for practice so they can truly engage and learn with digital texts.

Talk Books . . . All the Time

When people hear about books, television shows, and movie recommendations, they are much more likely to check them out. Many students are not naturally drawn to books in the same way they are to other media, so it is essential to talk about books to encourage reading. You don't necessarily have time to read all the books in your classroom library yourself, but you can talk about books, even if you haven't read them yet.

I often pull a stack of books, open to the first page, and read aloud an initial passage to students. Students then add to the My Book Stack chart (see figure 2.4, page 56) in their reader's notebook any book that sounds interesting. (See page 62 for a blank reproducible version of this figure.)

My Book Stack Chart				
Title	**Author**	**Recommended By**	**Brief Summary**	**Why I Might Like It**
Harry Potter and the Sorcerer's Stone	J. K. Rowling	My sister	Harry heads to Hogwarts School for Wizards to escape his mean aunt and uncle.	I have watched the movie, and my sister keeps telling me the book is way better.
Mind Gym	Gary Mack	My football coach	This book is about how our minds are more powerful than our bodies. Apparently, I can think my way to better football playing.	I want to eventually make the varsity team.
Catching Fire	Suzanne Collins	Me! I liked **The Hunger Games**, and this is the next one in the series.	Follows Katniss and Peeta after they won Hunger Games.	**The Hunger Games** was really good. I think this one will be, too.
Mockingjay	Suzanne Collins	Me! If I like **Catching Fire**, I will want to keep reading the series.	Not sure. Don't want to know anything yet until I read **Catching Fire**.	Unless **Catching Fire** isn't good, I will want to read this one, too.
Divergent	Veronica Roth	Dr. McCarty	It's dystopia. Reminded me of **The Hunger Games**, which I read and liked.	Dr. McCarty read an excerpt, and it sounds interesting. Lot of pages, though.

Figure 2.4: My book stack chart.

You can engage students in talking about books, too. I love Steven L. Layne's (2009) "Book Buzz" idea from *Igniting a Passion for Reading*. He provides open-ended prompts for students to discuss in small groups (Layne, 2009). Following are a few adaptations.

- What is the major problem in this book so far? How do you think it will be solved?

- Select a character in this book, and explain why you think the author created the character. How would the story change if the character was removed?

- Read aloud for your group the inside jacket flap or back cover. Discuss whether you feel the publisher has done an effective job of convincing people to read the book based on this information. What do your group members think?

What's great about this activity is that students don't have to be reading the same book to answer a question like, "Which character are you most connecting with, and why?" These discussions always lead to students getting new ideas about what book they want to be sure to read during the current semester.

Inviting influential adults into the classroom to talk about what they are reading not only "sells" potential next reads, but also demonstrates that reading is valuable, even cool. When the football coach talks about *Mind Gym: An Athlete's Guide to Inner Excellence* by Gary Mack (2001), students who are involved in any passion where they can sharpen their mind to affect performance will be motivated to pick up the book. Additionally, students see that reading has benefits outside the classroom and beyond high school graduation.

Support your colleagues and students in putting a book talk together. A book talk is a brief (one or two minutes) and often informal presentation with the goal of enticing others to read a book. When giving a book talk, your audience is going to be most interested in hearing about a book you found enjoyable or valuable to read. They also may be interested in:

- The title and author

- The genre

- A short introduction to the characters and setting

- A setup to the primary conflict in the text that creates intrigue

- Any challenges you faced with comprehension and how you overcame them

- Your opinion on who might like the book

Engaging book talks often include a very brief reading from the book. Find a portion of the text that doesn't spoil anything for the audience, but creates curiosity.

Getting Started

Consider the following suggestions as you immerse students in engaging, rich, and diverse texts.

1. **Ask students how they define *literacy* and *text*:** Start here! Then bridge their literacies with the academic literacy in your class. For example, ask students to storyboard the clever TikTok video they created over the weekend. Develop ways to shift their thinking and reflect on the literacy practices they engage in daily without even realizing it.

2. **Consider how your thinking has changed regarding the adolescent reader:** How has your thinking changed regarding the definitions of *literacy* and *text*? Consider sharing your "ahas" with students. Whenever you share a discovery or misconception you clarified, it shows students that you think while you read.

3. **Brainstorm nontraditional texts, such as paintings, artifacts, photographs, short films, or podcasts relevant to students, that you can use in instruction:** Consider giving students an opportunity to talk or write about their passion and point out the literacy skills they use to grow in their expertise of that passion. This could be a sport, activity, hobby, or academic subject. Engage in conversations with your content area colleagues about the texts they use in their classes, and encourage them to bridge students from nontraditional texts to academic texts.

4. **Get active on social media:** Are you using social media to bridge students' literacies? Open an X (formerly Twitter) account. Start a class Instagram account. If students like creating videos on TikTok, have them share with you what is trending, how they create their content, or how they think the platform could positively affect learning. There are many hashtags, organizations, authors, teacher librarians, and book sellers to follow. Even better, get students to follow their favorite authors and hashtags like #ownvoices and #weneeddiversebooks. You can try other social media platforms like Blue Sky, Clubhouse, Counter Social, Discord, Linked In, Mastodon, Threads, Reddit, Tumblr, or WT.Social. However, be sure to check out each site first to gauge its appropriateness for your grade level and age group.

5. **Clean out and update your classroom library:** What books are hanging out on your shelves that students haven't touched in years?

What books do you have that might misrepresent a population of students or perpetuate stereotypes? Weed them out!

6. **Find ways to use old books:** Do you have some old books that need to go? Keep some of these old books for black-out poetry—a great way to get students to look carefully at the written word and create something new. Students can create *black-out poetry* by taking a page or two from a book and then blacking out all the text except for the words they want to keep to create a poem or message. If you don't have any old books, ask your librarian.

7. **Find creative ways to "sell" books to future classes:** Do you need some help talking about and selling books to students? Have students create book trailers or advertisements for their favorite reads. This helps sell books to current and future students. Be sure to share when you've been "sold" a book. There is nothing better than when students see a teacher pick up a book because of their recommendation.

Conclusion

Surrounding students with texts isn't an easy task, but it is important if you want students to be motivated to read and persist through the productive struggle inevitable to the learning process. Not only should you bring texts into the classroom so they are near students, but you should also be intentional getting students to interact with and think about what they are reading.

The next chapter explores the inquiry approach to learning more deeply. In the process, I will discuss how to intentionally develop text sets to support that learning. Prioritizing texts in the classroom require you to advocate for funding and lean on the librarians in your community, teammates, and book vendors for support in curating the highest quality resources.

Comprehending a Tutorial

Tutorial video title: _____

Creator: _____

Video URL: _____

_____

I notice . . .

_____
_____
_____
_____
_____
_____
_____
_____
_____
_____
_____
_____
_____

I predict . . .

_____
_____
_____
_____
_____
_____
_____
_____
_____
_____
_____
_____

I am confused by . . .

I learned . . . , or I'm wondering . . .

I think the creator wants me to . . .

My Book Stack Chart

Title	Author	Recommended by	Brief Summary	Why I Might Like It

CHAPTER 3

Using Inquiry for English Language Arts and Literacy

During my first year of teaching, my colleague invited me to co-plan and implement a writing activity for our eleventh graders. Her idea was to create an elaborate crime scene with clues and evidence in her classroom, down the hallway, and into my classroom. Students would come in the next day with notebooks and make observations about what they saw, ensuring they didn't tamper with the evidence, since other students would also be collecting notes.

In setting up the crime scene, we came in after hours when all sports and activities had finished for the day. My colleague was creative, and her students adored her. She had all kinds of interesting items. She dipped a doll's feet in washable paint and made footprints from a partially open window, down the wall, across the room, down the hallway, into my classroom, and into a closet. I remember knocked-over plants, missing classroom items, ripped fabric, partially eaten snacks left lying on the windowsill, and messages written in some kind of code on the white boards. Most of all, I remember feeling uneasy and unsure how students were going to handle the observation day and if they would enjoy writing up their hypotheses, using evidence to back up their claims.

I was a more structured teacher, so this was definitely outside my comfort zone. However, I vividly remember the laughter, joy, and pure engagement of the students that day. They talked about the activity at lunch and in the hallways. It wasn't until about ten years later that I realized this colleague and mentor of mine was modeling inquiry, and we all were experiencing the benefits.

Chapters 1 and 2 introduced the concept of inquiry, but this chapter will further define inquiry and share practical ways you can use this approach in the classroom. Educators often think of inquiry in the context of science, where students are exploring the world, both natural and material, seeking to ask and answer questions, make discoveries, and construct new understanding. The Galileo Education Network (2015) defines *inquiry* as:

> A dynamic process of being open to wonder and puzzlement and coming to know and understand the world. Inquiry is based on the belief that understanding is constructed in the process of people working and conversing together as they pose and solve the problems, make discoveries and rigorously test the discoveries that arise in the course of shared activity.

This chapter explores using structured and guided inquiry in developing ELA or reading units of study. In ELA and literacy, we want students to wonder about how writers choose their genre and form when putting their words in print. We want students to make discoveries and puzzle through ideas while they are reading and collaborating. Reading, writing, and talking while immersed in a variety of texts representing multiple perspectives helps students know and understand the world. An inquiry approach requires the teacher to take on the roles of coach, facilitator, cheerleader, connector, challenger, and of course, teacher. We shift the ownership of learning from teacher to student.

While an inquiry approach to learning is prevalent in many classrooms, be sure you are implementing inquiry *intentionally*. Former OECD Global Project Manager of PISA 2018, Peter Adams (2021), states:

> The key lesson is that inquiry-based learning that is not teacher-centered and strongly scaffolded, and does not equip students with a tool kit, including fully worked examples, is likely to be successful only for those students who are already knowledgeable and well-skilled. For those who struggle with new information, the cognitive load might just overwhelm them.

For students to be in the driver's seat of their own learning, they need teachers to be intentional about deciding when to explicitly teach students. We are the experts, so students need us to model curating quality resources to guide their discovery. Students need educators who are responsive to their cognitive loads and can adjust with explicit instruction or letting go when appropriate. As educators, we need to discern when students are at their frustration level and are shutting down versus when they are persisting through productive struggle. When students lean toward shut down, we should step in and provide the support they require to keep learning. When students are struggling but persisting on their own, we need to step back and let go.

Considering the Inquiry Approach

When considering an inquiry approach to ELA and literacy instruction, educators are often concerned that the classroom will be too chaotic. Misconceptions that inquiry means a free for all, student choice all the time, and no teacher control can impede progress toward the more student-centered classroom environment that an inquiry approach provides. Instead, you can ease into inquiry. Leaders in the field of inquiry, Heather Banchi and Randy Bell (2008), introduce four levels of inquiry: (1) confirmation, (2) structured, (3) guided, and (4) open. While their context is science, the concepts can easily apply to the ELA classroom as well.

1. **Confirmation inquiry:** The teacher poses a question based on something students have already learned and then provides an activity in which students investigate that question to confirm their understanding.

2. **Structured inquiry:** The teacher and students work together to develop a set of essential or guiding questions, resources, and process of investigation to construct their understanding.

3. **Guided inquiry:** The teacher provides students with questions, and students create their own process for developing a plan and finding resources to answer the questions.

4. **Open inquiry:** Students generate their own questions and process of investigation, discovery, and sharing of new or refined knowledge (Banchi & Bell, 2008).

Similar to the four levels of inquiry, 3M and Google adopted the *genius hour*, in which the companies gave employees 20 percent of their time, or one day a week, to explore and develop something outside their day-to-day tasks (Farber, 2017).

Some educators have taken on a similar approach by giving students a genius hour to do open inquiry on whatever they are most interested in or have a passion for.

Figure 3.1 illustrates the types of inquiry you might use in an ELA classroom.

Confirmation Inquiry	Structured Inquiry	Guided Inquiry	Open Inquiry
Students confirm an already learned concept through investigation and answering teacher-generated questions.	Students investigate the answers to essential questions through carefully curated text sets already created by the teacher, teacher team, or curriculum.	Students investigate the answers to essential questions through a self-designed research process and self-selected texts. The teacher serves as the guide throughout the inquiry.	Students generate their own questions to explore and develop their process for investigation and sharing.
Example: Students review elements of fiction story structure. Students explore the wordless picture book *Journey* by Aaron Becker (2014). They then map the elements of fiction story structure from exposition to resolution as a way to answer the question, *How does this structure help the reader understand the story?*	**Example:** Students explore the essential question generated by the teacher: *How can literature promote social change?* Students receive a rich and diverse library of texts, including picture books, poetry, short stories, YA novels for book club, articles, video clips, and more, to interrogate the essential question through reading, writing, and discussion.	**Example:** Students explore the essential question: *What stories do artifacts tell and how do they help us understand our world?* Students explore museums of their choice and create a research plan to help them answer the question. In this case, either the teacher or the students determine how they will show what they have learned.	**Example:** Students receive a genius hour in which they can choose any question they are passionate about exploring, create and follow a research plan, and choose how to share what they have learned. The teacher provides an authentic audience for students to share their genius hour learning. This might include inviting caregivers (parents or guardians) in for a showcase, creating a public website, or bringing in community members to hear students share.

Figure 3.1: Inquiry continuum in ELA.

*Visit **go.SolutionTree.com/literacy** for a free reproducible version of this figure.*

Knowing you can step into inquiry whenever you are comfortable makes this approach more palatable for even the most resistant educator. If you are an educator who thrives in structure, you can start your inquiry journey at the confirmation level by making a slight adjustment to a lesson plan. For example, instead of giving a lecture on the structural elements of fiction, give a short minilesson and then ask students to explore picture books to identify the elements in an already published work.

Let's start our exploration of inquiry by understanding its importance for student learning. When we approach lesson planning and responding to students' needs and strengths from a place of curiosity, we can be more intentional and impactful in the classroom.

Embracing the Shift From Traditional to Inquiry-Based Instruction

Shifting your approach to ELA and literacy instruction can be challenging because, as English teachers, we may have experienced and been successful in a traditional ELA classroom in high school and in college. Making the switch to inquiry-based teaching provides an opportunity for so many more students to engage in ELA and literacy, providing reading, writing, speaking, listening, and language skills that benefit any career (Plucker, 2022b).

To illustrate the difference between traditional and inquiry approaches to ELA, see the example in figure 3.2.

Traditional Approach to ELA	Inquiry Approach to ELA
Novel Units Short Story Unit Poetry Unit Informational or Nonfiction Text Unit Vocabulary Research Paper Informative Speech Unit Oral Interpretation Unit Grammar	*What responsibilities do individuals have to contribute to society? What role does society play to better the individual?* **Inquiry Unit** • Book-club or seminar novel choices • Text set to include poetry, short story, informational text, and more • Speaking and writing focus: argument • Grammar, vocabulary, research, and collaboration integrated • Authentic opportunity to showcase learning: Create a constitution, mission statement, or bill of rights for the learning community.
	Is the opposite of love hate or indifference? **Inquiry Unit** • Anchor text: *Night* by Elie Weisel (2012)

Figure 3.2: Traditional versus inquiry approach to ELA.

continued →

- Book-club or seminar novel choices
- Text set to include poetry, short story, informational text, and more
- Writing focus: Narrative nonfiction or historical fiction
- Grammar, vocabulary, and speech integrated
- Authentic opportunity to showcase learning: Have the class interview an author who has published narrative nonfiction or historical fiction.

What role does storytelling play in our society?

Inquiry Unit

- Book-club or seminar novel choices
- Text set to include poetry, short story, informational text, and more
- Writing focus: memoir
- Speech focus: oral interpretation or storytelling
- Grammar, vocabulary, listening, and collaboration integrated
- Authentic opportunity to showcase learning: Conduct an oral storytelling event at a local elementary school and have students perform.

How do art, athletics, and literature affect social change?

Inquiry Unit

- Anchor text: *Raisin in the Sun* by Lorraine Hansberry (1959)
- Book-club or seminar novel choices
- Text set to include poetry, short story, informational text, and more
- Writing focus: advocacy
- Grammar, vocabulary, and speech integrated
- Authentic opportunity to showcase learning: Create a social media campaign to advocate for a social change issue of choice.

Students who have been educated in a traditional ELA classroom may resist the move to inquiry. They may have learned to be more passive, sitting in the "back seat" while their teacher drives the learning. Don't let that initial resistance hinder your work in implementing an inquiry approach. Before long, students will come to embrace the energy, joy, and sense of accomplishment that occurs when they are in control, constructing understanding, struggling and succeeding in productive ways, and embracing varied perspectives. Educators too can experience the same joy and accomplishment witnessing the growth of their students.

Implementing the Inquiry Approach in ELA Units

Deciding to integrate inquiry into ELA, reading, or literacy classes comes with challenges. You are letting students take the wheel, drive their own learning, and take their own routes to meet learning goals. To make this shift, it is beneficial to have a team of teachers to collaborate with to plan and implement an inquiry unit of study. Developing a healthy collaborative team takes time and effort, but the benefits are worth it.

While the process for developing ELA inquiry units of study is not linear, I will explore each element in detail in an order that promotes integrating learning goals and student ownership of learning. These elements include: braiding together learning goals, designing essential questions, and curating rich resources in text sets.

Figure 3.3 shows a unit map to support the process. It is built on the principles of understanding by design (UbD; Wiggins & McTighe, 2011) and the four critical questions addressed by collaborative teams in professional learning communities (PLCs; DuFour, DuFour, Eaker, Many, & Mattos, 2016). However, it is formatted in a way to support an inquiry approach to ELA unit design. (See page 96 for a blank reproducible version of this figure.)

Unit of Study: Community

Essential Questions:
- How do we define community?
- How can the individual positively impact the community?
- How can the community serve individuals?

Grade: 9

Time Frame:
First part of the school year, approximately four to six weeks, fifty-minute class period

1. What do I expect students to know and be able to do?	
Essential Learning (Standards): **Listening, Speaking, Viewing and Exchanging Ideas:** 9.3.1.2. Contribute to conversations by posing and responding to questions that relate the current discussion to broader themes or larger ideas; actively incorporate other into the discussion; and clarify, verify, or challenge ideas and conclusions, demonstrating preparation for the discussion.	**Learning Targets:** • The student can effectively contribute to conversations and ask and answer questions. • The student can come prepared for discussion. • The student can draw in others to the discussion.

Figure 3.3: ELA Inquiry unit of study example.

continued →

Reading:

9.1.2.3. Choose and read texts that address the purpose (e.g., personal interest, enjoyment, academic tasks).

9.1.4.1. Cite strong and thorough textual evidence to support conclusions of what a text says explicitly as well as inferences drawn from the text, including making connections to other texts; objectively summarize the text.

9.1.4.2. Analyze the themes or central ideas, including how they emerge and are shaped by specific details, of multiple texts, considering author perspective, identity, and bias.

9.1.5.1. Evaluate the impact of the author's use of literary elements on the structure of a text (e.g., narrator point of view, foreshadowing, pacing and flashbacks).

Writing:

9.2.5.2. Write to respond to a literary text, including analysis of narrative elements (e.g., writing personal reactions, analysis, and interpretation of text).

9.2.7.1. Formulate self-generated questions that guide inquiry to solve a problem, generating additional questions for further research and investigation.

Concepts and Vocabulary:

- Vocabulary: *community, culture, identity*
- Concepts: Textual shifts and impact

Audience and Purpose:

- Students will primarily consider each other and instructors in the classroom community as their audience, with the purpose of building healthy conditions for learning together throughout the rest of the school year.

Enduring Understandings:

- Students will understand that reading about the lives of others helps them understand themselves and their community.
- Students will learn how to behave as a member of a reading and writing community.

- The student can choose a text to read independently that they know they will enjoy discussing.
- The student can refer back to the text to back up what they say.
- The student can make connections from what they are reading to other texts they have read, listened to, or viewed.
- The student can determine the theme of the text and explain how that theme was developed.
- The student can effectively evaluate how an author constructs a story and uses elements such as point of view, foreshadowing, and flashbacks.
- The student can respond to what they are reading in their reader's response journal, sharing reactions, analysis, and interpretations of the texts.
- The student can ask questions to generate curiosity related to the unit's essential question, what they are reading, and in response to the class and book-club discussions.
- The student can do research to further investigate answers to the questions they generate.

2. How will I know they are learning it?

Formative Assessments:

- Exit cards asking for theme from shared picture book read alouds

Summative Assessments:

- Book club book theme illustration

- Zone independent reading rating scale and observations
- Writing about reading in readers' notebooks
- Creating anchor charts to establish community agreements
- Small-group discussion

- Book club discussion (Figure 3.9, page 91, illustrates a rubric that can be used for assessment book-club discussions.)
- Exemplary readers' notebook entries

3. What will I do if they aren't learning it or haven't learned it yet?

Strategies for Scaffolding and Intervention:
- Conferencing and reteaching
- Providing sentence frames
- Supplying examples of themes
- Giving opportunities for redos

4. What will I do if they already know it? What will I do when they learn it quickly?

Strategies for Enrichment:
- Steer advanced readers toward texts with greater complexity.
- Encourage independent inquiry and allow students to expand into research beyond the text set provided.
- Be open to new ideas for how students show their learning (for example, accept an alternative summative assessment if they want to show they understand story structure by writing an original piece).

Menu of Instructional Activities

(This is not a comprehensive list, but rather a set of ideas to illustrate how you can use materials to meet learning goals.)

START TOGETHER—Whole Group (Shared Text, Minilesson Ideas)

Read-Aloud Texts:
- *The Curious Garden* by Peter Brown serves as an opportunity for students to see what happens when they follow their curiosity. It also shows how modeling positive action can lead others to follow. Students can also identify literary devices such as personification and foreshadowing. Students may also discuss how illustrators enhance the message of the text.
- *14 Cows for America* by Carmen Agra Deedy creates an opportunity to discuss how and when tragedies occur (in this case, the terrorist attack on September 11th, 2001), communities come together, even from places far away, to provide support.
- *Chik Chak Shabbat* by Mara Rockliff offers an opportunity for students to see how individuals from different cultural backgrounds share commonalities, bringing them together in community.
- *The Name Jar* by Yangsook Choi illustrates the challenges with assimilation and invites students to consider experiences immigrants encounter in American schools. Can lead to positive discussions around how to honor and elevate cultural differences in our classroom community.
- Explore a current events article or news clip showing communities supporting one another. Asks students to identify the characteristics of community and discuss how those characteristics can be applied in a classroom community.

continued →

Minilesson Ideas:

- **Text Structure and Form**

  The Curious Garden by Peter Brown and *Community Gardens: Grow Your Own Vegetables and Herbs* by Susan Burns Chong can be used for a minilesson on form and author choice. One student chooses a fiction picture book to show the benefits of community gardens, while another chooses a more traditional nonfiction trade book. Students can make observations and identify the similarities and differences between the structure and content.

- **Community Norms or Common Agreements**

  Students can generate characteristics for how the class can operate as a healthy community of learners and compile on an anchor chart to hang in the classroom. This could come after watching Dontae Latson's 2017 TED Talk: *The Power of Community*.

- **Define "Reading Zone"**

  Have students generate a list of what it might look like, feel, and sound when they are "lost in a book." How do they manage distractions? What helps them get into a story and then stay engaged? What is stamina? Why is it necessary for maintaining focus while reading?

  Discuss the rating scale in the classroom engagement chart (figure 1.2, page 21). Ask students to describe what each rating would look, feel, and sound like in your classroom. Compile ideas on a shared document (digitally or on chart paper).

- Using any of the picture books, read and map the fiction story structure together.

GUIDED PRACTICE—Independent and Small-Group Ideas

- Have students choose a fiction or narrative nonfiction text from the class collection of picture books and map the fiction story structure in small groups.

- Read independently for twenty minutes and write about the reading in a reader-response journal for five minutes.

- Conduct reading conferences with individual students.

- Meet with small groups of students to conduct guided reading instruction.

END TOGETHER—Whole Group (Ideas for Sharing Learning)

- Use a digital collaboration tool to collect examples of how students managed distractions during independent reading time.

- Have students fill out an exit card sharing their engagement rating score (1–5) for independent reading during class that day and why. Students could also set a goal for the next day.

- Have student engage in book-club talks. Students can quickly go around the large-group circle and share what book they are reading and how they would rate it so far (out of five stars). Encourage students to be brief, so each student gets a chance to share before class ends.

- Ask students to define theme and explain what they believe the author has established as a primary theme for their book club book.

Text Set and Instructional Resources

Figure 3.6 (page 83) offers text sets for a ninth-grade ELA community inquiry unit. It includes a comprehensive list of picture books, nonfiction trade books, articles, speeches, infographics, videos, poetry, short stories, podcasts, book club options, and more.

Source: © 2020 by Mackin Learning. Used with permission.
Source: Adapted from DuFour, DuFour, Eaker, Many, & Mattos, 2016; Wiggins & McTighe, 2011.
Source for standards: Minnesota Department of Education, n.d.

STORIES FROM THE FIELD

I was beginning my second year as a teacher on special assignment (TOSA) at the central office. My first year, I was a K–12 intervention specialist who had spent the year immersing myself in elementary, middle, and high school classrooms to study the systems currently in place to support students' literacy growth. I was also on the district's multitiered systems of support (MTSS) team, working on continuous improvement in literacy. Prior to this role, I taught high school English and implemented ELA with an inquiry approach.

In year two, the district's literacy coordinator returned to the classroom, and our team of secondary ELA educators were left without someone to lead the revision process for ELA and the implementation of the Minnesota academic standards for ELA and literacy in science, social studies, and technical subjects (Minnesota Department of Education, n.d.).

My boss approached me and asked if I was interested or if I knew who might be. I proposed we do something unique. Knowing how important collaboration and collective inquiry is to change and recognizing the need to move to an inquiry approach in our secondary ELA classrooms, I asked if we could use the full-time salary for a literacy coordinator and, instead, hire English teachers to be ELA lead teachers paid by a stipend. I likened it to being a coach or an advisor. Many full-time teachers spend hours of additional time coaching football or debate and are compensated by a stipend. I knew we would find passionate ELA teachers to participate on a district-level collaborative team to redesign the curriculum and provide peer leadership for a stipend. So, we decided to try. We received many applicants and were able to put together a rock-star team of brilliant educators to lead this change.

My role in year two as a TOSA was to facilitate the group. We met twice a month after school for a few hours each time and quarterly for a full day out of the classroom, with substitutes provided. Knowing that our team would need to have honest dialogue, embrace dissonance, and lead peers, we began by learning together. This group learned all about inquiry in ELA and implemented in their own classrooms for six months before we pulled the ELA teaching community at large together to begin learning.

Braid Together Learning Goals

Educators often feel like they don't have time to create conditions for inquiry because the process of student discovery and construction of knowledge takes time, and there is never enough time to cover all the standards and other required curricular items. And in reality, when you approach learning thinking you need to *cover* standards, you can inadvertently shift from learning to teaching. If you are *covering* standards, you might design lesson plans ensuring your checklist of learning goals is part of the instruction but not necessarily integrate them into the guided practice students are engaging with or the assessments, both formative and summative.

However, when you integrate, or *braid*, learning goals across content areas, students will grow their ELA and literacy skills in a recursive and compounding way, which ultimately saves time (Plucker, 2022b). This time savings allows you to embrace inquiry and reap the benefits of student engagement, ownership, and mastery of standards. Most ELA standards documents include learning goals in these four strands.

1.   Reading, both literature and nonfiction

2.   Writing, in the forms of informative, argumentative, and narrative

3.   Speaking and listening, to include collaboration

4.   Conventions or language learning goals, which include grammar skills

In every inquiry unit of study, students should engage in reading, writing, and talking, so it makes sense to braid learning goals from across these strands. Educators also have learning goals that are not in the standards. Some have goals related to scholarship, such as meeting deadlines and supporting students in maintaining the stamina to accomplish difficult tasks. Some educators are part of magnet or theme-based school communities and are weaving STEM or leadership goals into their units of study. And others embrace the opportunity to set up students for navigating complex conversations on social change. When beginning to develop or refine units of study, a collaborative team can bring together all the learning goals needed for student achievement to create a comprehensive bank to pull from while writing these units.

When starting the process, a good exercise is to look through a list of required standards for your grade level, including any standards required by your state, recommended nationally, and mandated by your local curriculum, then determine which learning goals naturally work together. Let's see what this might look like for an ELA or literacy course. To illustrate, I will use the Common Core State Standards (CCSS; National Governors Association Center for Best Practices [NGA] & Council of Chief

State School Officers [CCSSO], 2010), as they are still utilized in some fashion in many U.S. states. If your state does not use CCSS, chances are your ELA learning goals are similar. You will notice that standards from reading, writing, speaking and listening, and language are included.

It's important to consider the ways these strands can work together in a unit of study. Then consider other goals that could be braided together. Some of these goals may come from standards provided by other organizations or goals that your collaborative team or school has deemed important for the development of scholars.

The example in figure 3.4 includes social justice standards from Learning for Justice (n.d.b), along with teacher-generated learning goals related to reading with stamina and free from distraction.

Essential Question: How can literature promote social change?		
Strand	**Standard**	**Key Elements to Braid**
Reading Literature	Analyze how an author's choices concerning how to structure a text, order events within it (e.g., parallel plots), and manipulate time (e.g., pacing, flashbacks) create such effects as mystery, tension, or surprise. (CCSS.ELA-LITERACY.RL.9–10.5)	Analyze author's choices concerning text structure.
Reading Literature	Determine a theme or central idea of a text and analyze in detail its development over the course of the text, including how it emerges and is shaped and refined by specific details; provide an objective summary of the text. (CCSS.ELA-LITERACY.RL.9–10.2)	Determine the central theme.
Writing	Write narratives to develop real or imagined experiences or events using effective techniques, well-chosen details, and well-structured event sequences. (CCSS.ELA-LITERACY.W.9–10.3)	Write narratives using effective technique.
Writing	Engage and orient the reader by setting out a problem, situation, or observation, establishing one or multiple point(s) of view, and introducing a narrator and/or characters; create a smooth progression of experiences or events. (CCSS.ELA-LITERACY.W.9–10.3. A)	Orient the reader through smooth progression of events.
Writing	Use narrative techniques, such as dialogue, pacing, description, reflection, and multiple plot lines, to develop experiences, events, and/or characters. (CCSS.ELA-LITERACY.W.9–10.3. B)	Use narrative techniques such as dialogue, pacing, and reflection.

Figure 3.4: Braiding learning goals in ELA.

continued →

Writing	Use a variety of techniques to sequence events so that they build on one another to create a coherent whole. (CCSS.ELA-LITERACY.W.9–10.3.C)	Use a variety of techniques to sequence events to create a coherent whole.
Speaking and Listening	Initiate and participate effectively in a range of collaborative discussions (one-on-one, in groups, and teacher-led) with diverse partners on grades 9–10 topics, texts, and issues, building on others' ideas and expressing their own clearly and persuasively. (CCSS.ELA-LITERACY.SL.9–10.1)	Participate effectively in collaborative discussions.
Speaking and Listening	Come to discussions prepared, having read and researched material under study; explicitly draw on that preparation by referring to evidence from texts and other research on the topic or issue to stimulate a thoughtful, well-reasoned exchange of ideas. (CCSS.ELA-LITERACY.SL.9–10.1. A)	Come to discussions prepared. Refer to evidence from texts.
Language	Apply knowledge of language to understand how language functions in different contexts, to make effective choices for meaning or style, and to comprehend more fully when reading or listening. (CCSS.ELA-LITERACY.L.9–10.3)	Apply knowledge to make effective choices for meaning and comprehend fully when reading and listening.
Diversity	I interact comfortably and respectfully with all people, whether they are similar or different from me. (DI.9–12.6)	Interact respectfully with all people.
Justice	I can recognize, describe and distinguish unfairness and injustice at different levels of society. (12 JU.9–12.12)	Recognize unfairness and injustice.
Action	I have the courage to speak up to people when their words, actions or views are biased and hurtful, and I will communicate with respect even when we disagree. (AC.9–12.18)	Speak up to people when words, actions, or views are biased. Communicate with respect, even during disagreements.
Scholar Behavior	I can actively read independently for twenty minutes at a time, maintaining stamina, managing and avoiding distractions. (9.5.10.10a)	Actively read, maintaining stamina and avoiding distractions.

Activities That Braid Learning Goals:

1. Students explore a shared narrative text and identify the decisions the author makes that follows features of narrative text structure. The text choice represents a theme related to social change, and students practice identifying the theme, recognizing unfairness, and practicing communication that is respectful, particularly in times of disagreement.

2. Students participate in book-club discussions practicing all the key elements to braid from this chart. Place students in book clubs based on a choice novel. The choice novels are examples of narrative text structure and represent themes related to social change.

3. Students, when given time to read during class, actively read their book with stamina for twenty minutes, devoid of any distractions, and monitoring and adjusting their comprehension.

4. Students practice the speaking and listening and learning for justice standards during book-club discussions.

5. Students write short pieces related to a social change issue of interest and passion using narrative features of dialogue, pacing, and sequencing into a coherent narrative whole. Through peer editing and teacher-writer conferences, students will improve writing and consider the important role conventions play for publishing and the ease of comprehension for the reader.

Example:

One group of high school students is reading *The 57 Bus* by Dashka Slater (2017), examining the narrative structure features, noticing that the author also weaves in other forms of writing such as poetry, text messages, letters, and informational text. Another group is reading *Long Way Down* by Jason Reynolds (2017), examining the features of narrative fiction, noticing that the author writes the entire novel in free-verse poetry.

Source for standards: Learning for Justice, n.d.b; Minnesota Department of Education, n.d.; NGA & CCSSO, 2010.

Beginning the process by braiding together learning goals gives you or your collaborative team an opportunity to focus on what students need to learn and do rather than what educators want to teach.

Design Essential Questions

One way you can pique students' curiosity for learning is through generating intriguing, essential questions for students. Essential questions are open-ended, prompting students to think deeply about a topic and discuss or even debate it. Focus on topics that interest and engage students. No longer do you need to approach a unit design conversation with the statement, "Today we're going to start our unit on *Of Mice and Men* by John Steinbeck." Instead, you can consider themes and essential questions to invite students into the process of reading, writing, and discussing your way through the novel and its themes.

This is a structured inquiry approach to unit development. You can develop unit questions that allow students to wrestle with ideas, seek perspectives in multiple texts, and revise thinking and learning for multiple weeks. When designing essential questions, authors Grant P. Wiggins and Jay McTighe (2011) recommend considering whether the questions lead to genuine and relevant inquiry into the big ideas for ELA, provoking lively discussion, more questions, and deep thought, and requiring students to weigh evidence, consider alternative ideas, and support and justify claims with evidence from text. Most important, essential questions should be provocative to adolescents—questions that relate to topics they are already passionate about or interested in.

Figure 3.5 (page 80) provides some examples of essential questions covering a variety of ELA topics and concepts (Staff, 2022).

Community and Citizenship

- How do actions and decisions of individuals affect the larger community?
- When is it okay to criticize your country or community?
- How can we debate or dialogue productively?
- What stories do artifacts tell and how do they help us understand our world?
- How do attitudes, values, and actions impact civic engagement?
- What is the individual's relationship to the environment?
- How does the physical environment shape the individual?
- What is individualism? What are the dangers of extreme individualism?
- What is the individual's responsibility to society?
- What is society's responsibility to the individual?

Social Change

- How can literature drive social change?
- What are the factors that create an imbalance of power within a culture?
- Can breaking the law or rules ever be justified?
- How are prejudice and bias created?
- How do we overcome prejudice and bias?
- What happens when people stay silent about injustices happening around them?
- What is the role of government to support and protect its citizens?
- Who should have the power to elect leaders and change laws?
- How do injustices in society impact the individuals?
- Is justice really blind?
- What constitutes a "free" society?
- Can we truly be free when others are not?
- What are the dynamics of change?
- How are systems of oppression formed, implemented, and dissolved?

Identity and Human Nature

- Is human nature inherently evil or good?
- What happens to mankind when evil is an influence?
- How can power influence and corrupt an individual?
- What are the constructs of my identity?
- Is identity fluid?
- What shapes our identity?
- What is the impact of society on identity?
- What effect do social or cultural norms have on growing up?
- How does identity influence belonging?
- How does identity influence how one navigates and views the world around them?
- How can an individual cross boundaries and defy the limits of their cultural, political, and national identities?

American Dream

- What is the American Dream?
- How do race, class, culture, and gender identity impact the American Dream?
- Is the American Dream desirable?
- Who has access to the American Dream?
- How does the desire for the American Dream infiltrate our consciousness?
- How does the definition of the American Dream differ for refugees, immigrants, and citizens?

Traditions
• When is tradition no longer feasible, reasonable, applicable, or logical?
• Who or what determines the nature of tradition?
• Who determines what traditions to follow and which ones to discard, and when?
• When does one create their own traditions?

Source: Adapted from Staff, 2022.

Figure 3.5: Essential questions for ELA inquiry units.

Visit **go.SolutionTree.com/literacy** *for a free reproducible version of this figure.*

When thinking about whether your essential question is going to be effective for a multi-week inquiry unit of study, ask yourself the following.

1. "Is this question provocative for students? Will they get excited about spending weeks interrogating it?" Go ahead and run the essential questions by students to see how they respond.

2. "Does this question lend itself to activities for which I can braid learning goals? Will students have enough to read, write, discuss, practice scholarship, and more, with this question?"

3. "Will this question spark lively conversation?"

STORIES FROM THE FIELD

I was working with a team of English teachers who were transforming their curriculum from a traditional approach—reading a novel, writing a literary analysis paper, and then moving on to the next novel or pause for a grammar, speech, or poetry unit—to an inquiry approach. These teachers were so inspired by the idea of braiding learning goals, writing a provocative student-friendly question, and curating texts in which to immerse students that they decided to call their new units *Inspired Units of Study.* This team of middle and high school teachers unleashed their brilliance, struggled productively, and developed some tried-and-true engaging units of study.

continued →

One day, a group of educators who taught sophomores were stuck on the unit they were working on. Their essential question was, "What rhetorical devices can best persuade and lead to change?" My first question to the team was, "Is that a teacher question, or the essential question for the unit of study?" They understood immediately that they missed the part about making sure students would be genuinely excited about spending weeks trying to answer the question. Through our discussion, I learned that they wanted students to hone their argument skills and collaborate with social studies colleagues to help students see the role they can play in advancing community. They also were hoping students could accomplish some of the speaking standards with this unit.

I learned that many students in their sophomore class had attended a youth summit in their city and came back on fire for advocacy. Many felt that youth were underestimated and wanted to prove that when adults listen to youth, they might just hear some innovative solutions to persistent problems. The team landed on the essential question, "The promise of our current generation: What will they contribute to advance our local, national, and global communities? What are they already contributing?"

Much better!

Curate Rich Resources in Text Sets

A traditional approach to choosing texts for an ELA classroom is to take the anchor text or novel the entire class is going to read and pair it with additional texts that provide more insight for the plot, setting, or characters in the novel. Educators might also choose texts to provide background on the author of the novel. While these texts can be important in providing the necessary context for comprehending the novel, this activity reinforces the idea that ELA is about reading novels that teachers like instead of focusing on what excites and interests students.

The Thomas B. Fordham Institute (2016) defines a *text set* as "collections of texts tightly focused on a specific topic. They may include varied genres (fiction, nonfiction, poetry, and so forth) and media (such as blogs, maps, photographs, art, primary-source documents, and audio recordings)." You can more broadly define *text* to include photographs, charts, picture books, poetry, excerpts, infographics, articles, blogs, satirical cartoons, songs, podcasts, TED Talks, and more. Any piece of produced communication that provides an opportunity for thought, discussion, dissonance, and discovery can be considered a text to include in the curated resources for the unit of study.

So, what if you curated resources that allow students to immerse themselves in the theme of the unit and interrogate the essential question driving it? By doing so, you naturally shift from teaching a book to helping students master standards. An additional benefit of generating a text set to support the development of standards is that the process sets up the opportunity to offer more choice, which is a key strategy for student engagement (Guthrie & Klauda, 2014).

Figure 3.6 shows a completed text set chart for a ninth-grade ELA unit on community. The school librarian or media specialist is a valuable resource for gathering these text ideas. (See page 101 for a blank reproducible version of this figure.)

Ninth-Grade ELA Unit on Community Text Set Chart	
Essential Questions: • How do we define community? • How can the individual positively impact the community? • How can the community serve individuals?	
Anchor Text (if applicable): No whole class novel is used during this unit; instead, students have the choice to read a book independently or read a book in a small book-club group.	
Context: The purpose of the unit is to build a community of readers, writers, thinkers, and learners and understand the impact the individual can make in local, national, and global communities. This unit is a launch into the school year. During this unit of study, the teacher spends time introducing the procedures and routines for whole-group, independent, and collaborative work. This unit includes a focus on developing kindness and civility (bullying awareness) that is called for in this state's legislation at every grade level. Additionally, this unit focuses on several of the ninth-grade benchmarks legislated through the academic standards for ELA. Through this inquiry unit of study, students will have several opportunities to hone their skills in reading, writing, language, and speaking, viewing, and listening benchmarks.	
Types of Texts	**Possible Texts**
Picture Books	*14 Cows for America* by Carmen Agra Deedy (2018) *Energy Island* by Allan Drummond (2011) *The Curious Garden* by Peter Brown *Chik Chak Shabbat* by Mara Rockliff (2016) *The Name Jar* by Yangsook Choi (2013) *Community Soup* by Alma Fullerton (2023)

Figure 3.6: Example text set for ninth-grade ELA community inquiry unit.

continued →

Nonfiction Trade Books and Collections of Stories, Essays, or Poetry	*All Out: The No-Longer-Secret Stories of Queer Teens Throughout the Ages* by Saundra Mitchell (2020)
	Ants Work Together by Nora Ellison (2018)
	Black Enough: Stories of Being Young and Black in America by Ibi Zoboi (2020)
	Build Strong Communities by Maribel Valdez Gonzalez (2022)
	Civic Roles in the Community: How Citizens Get Involved by Cassandra Richards (2018)
	Community Gardens: Grow your Own Vegetables and Herbs by Susan Burns Chong (2014)
	Community Service and Volunteering by Marco Andres (2018)
	Freedom Walkers: The Story of the Montgomery Bus Boycott by Russell Freedman (2009)
	The Hill We Climb by Amanda Gorman (2021)
	Girl Rising: Changing the World One Girl at a Time by Tanya Lee Stone (2019)
	If the World Were a Village: A Book about the World's People by David Smith (2011)
	Kid Trailblazers: True Tales of Childhood from Changemakers by Robin Stevenson (2022)
	Real Kids, Real Stories, Real Character: Choices That Matter Around the World by Garth Sundem. (2016)
	A Teen Guide to Being Eco in Your Community by Cath Senker (2021)
	We are Power: How Nonviolent Activism Changes the World by Todd Hasak-Lowy (2022)
	You Can Too! Change the World by Monika Davies (2018)
Articles	"Kansas Students Stand Up to Hate, Bigotry in Push to Replace Klan Leader's Name" by Sherman Smith (2021)
TED Talks	Dontae Latson (2017) TED Talk: *The Power of Community*
News Clips	"Paradise Football Team Rises Again After California's Deadliest Wildfire Spared Its Field" by Scott Stump (2021)
	"It's More Than the Machinery: Farmers Come Together To Help Family in Need" by CBS News Minnesota (2021)
Poems	"The Hill We Climb" by Amanda Gorman (2021)
Short Stories	"Thank you, Ma'am" by Langston Hughes (2014)
	"Marigolds" in *Breeder and Other Stories* by Eugenia Collier (1994)
	"The Lottery" by Shirley Jackson (1948)
	"Amir" in *Seedfolks* by Paul Fleischman (2013)
Podcasts	*Which Towns Are Worth Saving?* with host Michael Barbaro (2021)
Independent Reading or Book-Club Choices	*The Boy Who Harnessed the Wind* by William Kamkwamba and Bryan Mealer (2009)
	Three Little Words by Ashley Rhodes-Courter (2008)
	I Am Malala by Malala Yousafzai (2015)
	The Power of Half: One Family's Decision to Stop Taking and Start Giving Back by Kevin Salwen and Hannah Salwen (2010)

	Revenge of a Not-So-Pretty Girl by Carolita Blythe (2013)
	Home Is Not a Country by Safia Elhillo (2021)
	Long Way Down by Jason Reynolds (2017)
	Three Things I Know by Betty Culley (2020)
Speeches	"2019 Commencement Speeches Call for Community, Kindness, and Critical Thinking" from The Alexander Group (2019)

The benefit of using multiple texts, especially short ones, is that it exposes students to varied perspectives, points of view, forms, and genres that provide multiple opportunities to interrogate the essential question, investigate the concept being explored, and further inquire about the topic. If, for example, you are exploring the meaning of the American Dream, you can choose stories written by refugees; immigrants; Americans from rural, suburban, and urban areas; and individuals with various cultural backgrounds. And because the texts are short, students are exposed to many more perspectives from which to answer the question.

When you choose to spend your entire unit on just one novel, you limit the exploration to one perspective. Certainly, students can be immersed in a novel, whether it is a whole-class novel, a book-club choice, or an independent reading book, which will give students an in-depth look at one perspective; but think how rich the experience is when placed against the backdrop of these multiple perspectives.

The beauty of a diverse text set is that it allows for immersion. Students can begin with these carefully curated texts to investigate the essential questions, wrestle with varying perspectives, and generate new questions. When you are ready to order texts for your inquiry unit, it is helpful to consider your purpose for each text as well as questions for determining the quantity of each text to order.

Figure 3.7 (page 86) provides an example of questions teaching teams might consider as they put together purchase requests for inquiry unit resources. (See page 105 for a blank reproducible version of this figure.)

Ultimately, having a rich text set can lead students to search for additional texts and perspectives, so they build new understandings, all while practicing and growing reading, writing, language, and collaboration skills.

Unit Theme and Essential Questions
Ninth-Grade ELA Unit on Community

What are the overarching essential questions for this unit?
- How do we define community?
- How can the individual positively impact the community?
- How can the community serve individuals?

What are your primary ELA goals?

Our goals are to get students reading independently for enjoyment, writing about what they are reading, helping them monitor comprehension and maintain their stamina for daily reading, and helping them have authentic and academic conversations about what they are reading. Through the process, our goal is to create a healthy classroom community of learners.

Anchor Text

Will students be reading an anchor text or whole-class novel? If so, which one?

We are not using a whole-class novel or anchor text for this unit.

(One copy of anchor text per student)

Anchor text title and author:

Number of students:

Book Study or Literature Circle

Will students be in small groups reading a text? If yes: Yes

Total number of students per section: Thirty-six students per class on average

Number of sections: Four sections of English 9

Group size: Four to six students per group

(I recommend having seven or eight text choices for students that represent a range of reading levels, with six copies of each title per class; thirty-six to forty-eight total books per section or class.)

Book-club title and author options:
- *The Boy Who Harnessed the Wind* by William Kamkwamba and Bryan Mealer (2009)
- *Three Little Words* by Ashley Rhodes-Courter (2008)
- *I Am Malala* by Malala Yousafzai (2015)
- *The Power of Half: One Family's Decision to Stop Taking and Start Giving Back* by Kevin Salwen and Hannah Salwen (2010)
- *Revenge of a Not-So-Pretty Girl* by Carolita Blythe (2013)
- *Home Is Not a Country* by Safia Elhillo (2021)
- *Long Way Down* by Jason Reynolds (2017)
- *Three Things I Know* by Betty Culley (2020)

Independent Reading

Will students be reading independently during this unit? Yes

Do you want them to read an independent novel related to the essential questions?

This isn't necessary since we have book-club options.

If *yes*, consider finding or purchasing:

(Two or three choices per student; one or two copies of each title)

Number of students _____ x 2.5 books = _____ total number of titles

Short Texts for Start Together and Interactive Read Aloud

In order to have a menu of options for shared conversations about the essential question, I recommend twenty to twenty-five texts (some can be open educational resources and do not need to be purchased) to choose from over the course of one inquiry unit of study. These should be short texts to be read aloud: poetry, picture books, articles, video clips, and so on.

- *14 Cows for America* by Carmen Agra Deedy (2018)
- *Energy Island* by Allan Drummond (2011)
- *The Curious Garden* by Peter Brown
- *Chik Chak Shabbat* by Mara Rockliff (2016)
- *The Name Jar* by Yangsook Choi (2013)
- *Community Soup by* Alma Fullerton (2023)
- *"Kansas Students Stand Up to Hate, Bigotry in Push to Replace Klan Leader's Name" by Sherman Smith (2021)
- *Dontae Latson (2017) TED Talk: *The Power of Community*
- *"Paradise Football Team Rises Again After California's Deadliest Wildfire Spared Its Field" by Scott Stump (2021)
- *"It's More Than the Machinery: Farmers Come Together to Help Family in Need" by CBS News Minnesota (2021)
- "The Hill We Climb" by Amanda Gorman (2021)
- "Thank you, Ma'am" by Langston Hughes (2014)·
- "Marigolds" in *Breeder and Other Stories* by Eugenia Collier (1994)
- "The Lottery" by Shirley Jackson (1948)
- "Amir" in *Seedfolks* by Paul Fleischman (2013)
- *Which Towns Are Worth Saving?* with host Michael Barbaro (2021)
- *"2019 Commencement Speeches Call for Community, Kindness, and Critical Thinking" from The Alexander Group (2019)
- *Open educational resources that are free and accessible for teachers

(One copy per teacher)

Guided Practice Texts

Will students be doing research or inquiry around the essential question during this unit? Yes

What topics need to be explored?

(I recommend one to three books per subtopic or concept available for small group or independent inquiry; fifteen to twenty books per research bin; one research bin per teacher.)

- *All Out: The No-Longer-Secret Stories of Queer Teens Throughout the Ages* by Saundra Mitchell (2020)
- *Ants Work Together* by Nora Ellison (2018)
- *Black Enough: Stories of Being Young and Black in America* by Ibi Zoboi (2020)
- *Build Strong Communities* by Maribel Valdez Gonzalez (2022)
- *Civic Roles in the Community: How Citizens Get Involved* by Cassandra Richards (2018)
- *Community Gardens: Grow Your Own Vegetables and Herbs* by Susan Burns Chong (2014)
- *Community Service and Volunteering* by Marco Andres (2018)
- *Freedom Walkers: The Story of the Montgomery Bus Boycott* by Russell Freedman (2009)

Figure 3.7: Questions to guide quantity decisions for inquiry text sets.

continued →

- *Girl Rising: Changing the World One Girl at a Time* by Tanya Lee Stone (2019)
- *If the World Were a Village: A Book About the World's People* by David Smith (2011)
- *Kid Trailblazers: True Tales of Childhood from Changemakers* by Robin Stevenson (2022)
- *Real Kids, Real Stories, Real Character: Choices That Matter Around the World* by Garth Sundem. (2016)
- *A Teen Guide to Being Eco in Your Community* by Cath Senker (2021)
- *We Are Power: How Nonviolent Activism Changes the World* by Todd Hasak-Lowy (2022)
- *You Can Too! Change the World* by Monika Davies (2018)

What Is Your Purpose?

Independent reading—Two or three choices per student

Book club—Sets of four to six copies of each title per class, seven or eight title choices

Anchor text or whole-class novel—One copy per student

Interactive read aloud—One copy per teacher

Research—One copy of each title (two or three titles per subtopic or concept, twenty to twenty-five total books) per research or inquiry bin

Assessing Students in Inquiry Units

When engaged in inquiry units of study, educators have many opportunities to check on student learning through formative assessment. Thinking about assessment using an athletic analogy can be helpful (Tovani, 2011). All day, every day, students practice (formative) for game day (summative). For example, consider a unit in which students participate in book clubs or seminar novel discussion groups. Students should know exactly what they will be graded on in a final discussion and have the opportunity to practice collaborating. And you want students to authentically learn from one another as they are reading the text and achieving mastery of learning goals.

Figure 3.8 shows a discussion rubric students could use as a self-assessment or peer evaluation following a collaborative discussion day. This is the summative assessment rubric as well, so students know exactly what they will be assessed on when their group has a graded discussion.

In an inquiry approach to ELA and literacy, teachers can more easily serve as coach. As students are reading, writing, and discussing their way to a greater understanding of their unit theme and essential question as well as the standards they are working to master, the teacher can gather information to see exactly where students are thriving and where they might be stuck and need help. Figure 3.9 (page 91) provides ideas for formative assessments that work well in an inquiry-based ELA or literacy course.

Book Club (Literature Circles / Authentic Small-Group Discussion)

Rubric for Evaluation:

Check one: _____ Formative _____ Summative

Check one: _____ Self _____ Peer _____ Teacher

Name: _____ Hour: _____

Learning Goal	1—Does Not Meet Expectations	2—Developing	3—Proficient	4—Exemplary
The student can complete the scheduled reading and demonstrate close reading.	Rarely completes assigned reading on schedule. Shows little to no evidence of close or annotated reading.	Sometimes has assigned reading completed on schedule. Shows little evidence shown of close or annotated reading.	Almost always has assigned reading completed on schedule. Shows several pieces of evidence of close or annotated reading.	Has assigned reading completed on schedule. Shows thoughtful, thorough pieces of evidence of close or annotated reading.
The student can work with peers to set and adhere to guidelines (norms) for their book discussion.	Demonstrates little understanding of agreed-upon norms. Lacks participation in creating norms. Breaks norms.	Participates some in developing norms. Understands agreed-upon norms but doesn't always adhere to them.	Actively participates in developing norms. Illustrates adherence to the agreed-upon norms. Occasionally holds peers accountable for agreed-upon norms.	Actively participates and provided leadership in developing norms. Boldly and confidently illustrates adherence to and holds peers accountable to agreed-upon norms.
The student can participate in a productive, authentic, text-dependent discussion with peers.	Does not participate in group discussions. Offers few opinions and makes no comments referring to the text, illustrating a close reading.	Participates reluctantly in group discussions. Offers few opinions and makes limited comments referring to the text, illustrating a close reading.	Participates competently in group discussions. Offers some insightful comments referring to the text, illustrating a close reading.	Participates enthusiastically in group discussions. Offers insightful and thoughtful comments referring to the text, illustrating a close reading.

Figure 3.8: Small-group book discussion rubric.

continued →

Learning Goal	1—Does Not Meet Expectations	2—Developing	3—Proficient	4—Exemplary
The student can propel conversations forward through posing and responding to questions related to the text.	Doesn't ask questions.	Asks few questions, but some are closed-ended questions (very plot focused).	Will occasionally ask thoughtful questions.	Asks pertinent, thoughtful questions that extend beyond the text.
The student can demonstrate active listening skills during small-group discussion.	Has difficulty paying attention to the speaker.	Listens occasionally but doesn't interact much with the information and group.	Listens carefully for information and comments occasionally.	Listens to other people's ideas. Stacks on or builds off others' ideas.
The student can discuss effectively and authentically what is in the text, about the text, and beyond the text with their group.	Shows little understanding of the text at any level of comprehension or relies heavily on literacy comprehension. Does not ask for clarification from peers.	Shows some understanding of the text at more than a literal level of comprehension. Does not seek to clarify misconceptions that may be hindering comprehension.	Shows understanding of the text at all levels of comprehension. Helps the group see beyond the literal and into application and synthesis of the text. Is able to help students clarify misconceptions that may hinder comprehension.	Shows a strong and thorough understanding of the text at all levels of comprehension. Helps the group see beyond the literal and into application and synthesis of the text. Is able to help students clarify misconceptions that may hinder comprehension.

Visit go.SolutionTree.com/literacy for a free reproducible version of this figure.

Formative Assessment	What We Might Learn
Class Engagement Chart	• What types of books students are reading • Student patterns for choosing and abandoning books • Student stamina for independent reading
Conferring Notes	• Skills in managing distractions • Stamina for independent work • Student comprehension strategies • Student mastery of learning goals • Misconceptions
Annotations	• Comprehension strategies • Misconceptions • Thinking within, about, and beyond the text
Reader-Response Journal Entries	• Thinking within, about, and beyond the text • Preferences for genre, form, authors, and topics • Connections with the text • Critique of text • Misconceptions
Discussion Observation Notes	• Collaboration skills for individuals • Roles individuals play in small-group discussion • Types of questions posed during discussion • Opportunities for student intervention or enrichment • How prepared students are for discussion
Discussion Rubric as Self- or Peer Feedback	• Where individuals are at with learning goals • How effectively groups are collaborating
Writing Drafts	• Where students are at with mastery of learning goals • Information to support guided writing groups or one-on-one writing conferences
Exit Cards	• Misconceptions • New learning • Where students might be stuck
Sticky Notes	• Thinking within, about, and beyond the text • Connections with the text • Critique of text • Misconceptions
Storyboard or Other Planning Tool	• Students' thinking processes for writing or creating of a digital or visual product • Information to support targeted instruction in small groups or individually to support mastery of learning goals • Progress toward final product

Figure 3.9: Formative assessments in an inquiry-based ELA course.

Throughout the inquiry unit, students should know that you "grade the learning, not the knowing" (Harvey & Daniels, 2015, p. 319). Inquiry is rooted in the idea that teachers focus on the process more than the product. This means you should reward students for the learning and thinking they are doing along the way.

Students will have misconceptions. Students will be partially right as they construct new understandings. You want students to know that this is part of the learning process, and if you only grade the right answer, you miss the opportunity to help students see that learning is about making mistakes, clarifying misunderstandings, and applying new learning in messy ways.

Supporting Students During Inquiry

Students will inevitably fall, fail, and flounder during their inquiry journey. Our role as educators is to support them in their growth. We want to ensure that all students grow, which means we need to look for the misconceptions, learning goals to target, and opportunities to push *all* students forward.

Sometimes when learning comes easy for a student, we inadvertently allow them to coast through class. We have a responsibility to create conditions in which all students experience the productive struggle of learning. Barbara Blackburn (2018) describes *productive struggle* as follows.

> The 'sweet spot' between scaffolding and support. Rather than immediately helping students at the first sign of trouble, we should allow them to work through struggles independently before we offer assistance. That may sound counterintuitive, since many of us assume that helping students learn means protecting them from negative feelings of frustration. But for students to become independent learners, they must learn to persist in the face of challenge.

We do a disservice to our high-achieving students if they aren't provided opportunities for growth. And we send the wrong message to students who find learning challenging if they don't see productive struggle from *all* their peers, especially those who seem to always "get it." Learning doesn't always come easy, and that is the wrong message to send.

STORIES FROM THE FIELD

When I made the shift to inquiry in my ELA classroom, I had to shift how I assessed student work. In one instance, my sophomores were drafting informational essays on a topic they were passionate about exploring. Students were writing on topics such as the following.

- Including girls on the school's wrestling and football teams

- Switching from a meat-based diet to vegan

- Recognizing the inherent biases of school dress codes

- Emphasizing attending trade or technical schools rather than a traditional four-year university

- Offering esports as a competitive activity in area schools

It was so much fun to give students the choice to research their topic, discuss it with me in conferences and with their peers in writing groups, and see their arguments take shape. I was able to use many formative assessment tools, such as a research planning document, annotations of research articles, outline drafts, and writing conference notes, to assess students on the unit's learning goals.

I made the shift to recording the learning in the gradebook as soon as I saw mastery. I didn't wait until the final paper. Another shift I made was to push gifted writers to grow. This was especially tough for one student, Nicole, who felt like an early draft was good enough for me to enter as the grade. Our conversation went something like this:

Nicole: "I feel good about my paper. I think I am done."

Me: "You should feel good about this draft. It has a strong, well-developed argument. You chose supporting details that not only appeal to our logic (logos), but also our emotions (pathos). And you establish the credibility (ethos) with all the expert quotes you include."

Nicole: "Great. So, am I done?"

continued →

Me: "My goal is for every student to grow in their writing. Your growth area is in your word choice and style. I see opportunities for you to employ some rhetorical devices, such as alliteration, reversals, or analogy, to make this even stronger."

Nicole: "So I can't use this as my final paper?"

Me: "No. This is a draft. I look forward to you pushing yourself to revise and make it even stronger."

Nicole may have rolled her eyes, but in the end, she pushed herself to research rhetorical devices, find the places in her paper where she wanted more emphasis, and apply stylistic changes. She was very proud of her final paper. Why? Because she was pushed to her productive struggle. We feel the best when we come out the other side of that struggle. Plus, I think Nicole appreciated that I believed she could be an even better writer.

Getting Started

Consider the following suggestions for implementing inquiry-based instruction in your ELA classroom.

1. **Consider starting small with a mini inquiry unit:** If you're new to inquiry, take one week for this mini inquiry, and have students explore an essential question and share their learning at the end of the week. Or try dedicating one day per week to a genius hour in which students can explore an interest or passion, design their own inquiry, and share their products or findings.

2. **Gather your collaborative team, or create one, and do a book study:** In addition to this book, others you might consider include *Empower: What Happens When Students Own Their Learning* by John Spencer and A. J. Juliani (2017), *Comprehension and Collaboration: Inquiry Circles for Curiosity, Engagement, and Understanding* by Stephanie Harvey and Harvey "Smokey" Daniels (2015), or *So What Do They Really Know?* by Cris Tovani (2011).

3. **Create a text set with an anchor text:** Take an anchor text or whole class novel you have had students read in the past, or you plan to

use soon, and create a text set with opportunities for students to explore a theme and essential question through various forms, genre, and perspectives.

4. **Conduct an assessment audit:** Ask yourself, "Do my assessments foster creativity? Do they reward process over product? Do they really show where students are on their journey to mastering braided learning goals?"

Conclusion

Much of this chapter focused on creating full inquiry units of study. While I think organizing ELA into more extensive units that span several weeks is an effective way to teach students, I also am aware that it isn't easy—or even allowed in some places—to revamp curriculum and lessons.

When working with a group of fourth-grade teachers required to use the district's purchased curriculum, we looked at each unit and considered the principles outlined in this chapter. The unit they wanted to improve wasn't engaging students in the way they had hoped. So we supplemented with a few texts that were more engaging, looked for ways to offer more choice, and shifted the structure to follow a workshop approach—start together, guided practice, end together—which will be discussed in further detail in the next chapter. The team realized they could follow the curriculum provided while layering an inquiry approach over the top.

The point is, use the inquiry approach in the way it works best in your school and your classroom. Every situation is different. Inquiry allows flexibility in instruction and student participation. Use your expertise to weave inquiry into your existing curriculum to meet the requirements of your school or district as well as the needs of your students.

ELA Inquiry Unit of Study Template

Unit of Study: _____

Essential Questions:

_____

_____

_____

_____

Grade: _____   **Time Frame:** _____

1. What do I expect students to know and be able to do?

Essential Learning (Standards):	Learning Targets:
_____	_____
_____	_____
_____	_____
_____	_____
_____	_____
_____	_____
Reading:	_____
_____	_____
_____	_____
_____	_____
_____	_____
_____	_____
_____	_____
Writing:	_____
_____	_____
_____	_____
_____	_____
_____	_____
_____	_____

Audience and Purpose:

_____

_____

_____

_____

_____

_____

Concepts and Vocabulary:

_____

_____

_____

_____

_____

_____

_____

_____

_____

Enduring Understandings:

_____

_____

_____

_____

_____

_____

_____

_____

_____

2. How will I know they are learning it?

Formative Assessments:	**Summative Assessments:**
_____	_____
_____	_____
_____	_____
_____	_____
_____	_____
_____	_____
_____	_____
_____	_____
_____	_____
_____	_____
_____	_____
_____	_____

3. What will I do if they aren't learning it or haven't learned it yet?

Strategies for Scaffolding and Intervention:

---

4. What will I do if they already know it? What will I do when they learn it quickly?

Strategies for Enrichment:

Menu of Instructional Activities

(This is not a comprehensive list but rather a set of ideas to illustrate how you can use materials to meet learning goals.)

START TOGETHER—Whole Group (Shared Text, Minilesson Ideas)

Read-Aloud Texts:

_____

_____

_____

_____

_____

_____

_____

_____

_____

_____

_____

_____

_____

Minilesson Ideas:

_____

_____

_____

_____

_____

_____

_____

_____

_____

_____

_____

_____

_____

_____

_____

_____

_____

Guided Practice—Independent and Small-Group Ideas

_____
_____
_____
_____
_____
_____
_____
_____
_____
_____

END TOGETHER—Whole Group (Ideas for Sharing Learning)

_____
_____
_____
_____
_____
_____
_____
_____
_____
_____
_____
_____

Text Set and Instructional Resources

_____
_____
_____
_____
_____

Source: © 2020 Mackin Learning. Used with permission.

Source: Adapted from DuFour, R., DuFour, R., Eaker, R., Many, T., & Mattos, T. (2016). Learning by doing: A handbook for Professional Learning Communities at Work (3rd ed.). Bloomington, IN: Solution Tree Press; Wiggins, G. P., & McTighe, J. (2011). The understanding by design guide to creating high-quality units. Alexandria, VA: Association of Supervision and Curriculum Development.

Source for Standards: Minnesota Department of Education. (n.d.). English language arts standards. Accessed at https://education.mn.gov/mde/dse/stds/ela on July 5, 2023.

My Text Set Chart

Essential Questions:

_____

_____

_____

_____

Anchor text (if applicable): _____

Context: _____

_____

Types of Texts	Possible Texts
Picture Books	
Nonfiction Trade Books	
Articles	
TED Talks	

Infographics	
Statistics or Graphs	
Definitions	
Short Films	
Photographs	
News Clips	

Songs	
Poems	
Short Stories	
Graphic Novel Excerpts	
Podcasts	
Audiobook Clips	

Speeches	
Other	

Questions to Guide Quantity Decisions for Inquiry Text Sets

Unit Theme and Essential Questions

What are the overarching essential questions for this unit?

_____

_____

_____

What are your primary ELA goals?

_____

_____

_____

_____

_____

_____

_____

_____

_____

_____

_____

_____

_____

_____

_____

Anchor Text

Will students be reading an anchor text or whole-class novel? If so, which one?

_____

_____

(One copy of anchor text per student)

Anchor text title and author:

_____

_____

Number of students: _____

Book Study or Literature Circle

Will students be in small groups reading a text? If *yes*: _____

Total number of students per section: _____

Number of sections: _____ **Group size:** _____

(I recommend having seven or eight total choices for students with texts that represent a range of reading levels, with six copies of each title per class; thirty-six to forty-eight total books per section or class.)

Book-club title and author options:

_____

_____

_____

_____

_____

_____

_____

_____

_____

_____

_____

_____

_____

_____

_____

Independent Reading

Will students be reading independently during this unit?

_____

Do you want them to read an independent novel related to the essential questions? If *yes*, consider finding or purchasing:

_____

_____

_____

_____

_____

(Two or three choices per student; one or two copies of each title)

Number of students _____ x 2.5 books = _____ total number of titles

Short Texts for Start Together and Interactive Read Aloud

In order to have a menu of options for shared conversations regarding the essential question, I recommended having twenty to twenty-five texts to choose from over the course of one inquiry unit of study. These should be short texts to be read aloud: poetry, picture books, articles, video clips, and so on. (One copy per teacher)

_____

_____

_____

_____

_____

_____

_____

_____

_____

_____

Guided Practice Texts

Will students be doing research or inquiry around the essential question during this unit?

_____

What topics need to be explored?

(I recommended having one to three books per subtopic or concept available for small group or independent inquiry; fifteen to twenty books per research bin)

_____

_____

_____

_____

_____

_____

_____

_____

What Is Your Purpose?

Independent reading—Two or three choices per student

Book club—Sets of four to six copies of each title per class, seven or eight title choices

Anchor text or whole-class novel—One copy per student

Interactive read aloud—One copy per teacher

Research—One copy of each title (two or three titles per subtopic or concept, twenty to twenty-five total books) per research or inquiry bin

CHAPTER 4

Structuring Class Time for Authentic Literacy Engagement

When I first started implementing a workshop framework, I struggled to keep to the times associated with the three parts: fifteen minutes for whole-group "start together," in which we participated in a minilesson or read aloud; twenty-five minutes for guided practice, in which students worked in small groups or independently; and five to ten minutes to "end together" as a class, in which students shared and reflected on the day's learning. I was excited when students were attentive during the minilesson and often allowed myself to keep going, soon realizing half the class time was over. Or students would be so into their books, reading silently, that I would let them read to the bell.

As we explore in this chapter, sticking to the rhythm and time frame for each part of the workshop is essential because each part plays a specific role. The minilesson is designed to target specific skills and goals the majority of students need. Guided practice is for the intent purpose of meeting individual needs and providing time for targeted instruction for small groups of students. Sharing provides important formative assessment data for adjusting the next day's lesson and holding students accountable for what they accomplished during their independent or small-group time.

I realized I needed a tool to help me stay on schedule. I found a visual timer online that I could set; and as a group, we could see how much time we had left, and it would alarm when time was up. I set that timer for fifteen-, twenty-five-, and ten-minute intervals. If I forgot, students would jump at the chance to keep us on schedule. This meant I had to let go of "finishing" tasks. It became OK to not finish a picture book and come back to it the next day or leave a small group with tasks to try on their own because it was time for me to move to another group or pull everyone back together for sharing.

This chapter first describes the workshop framework in more detail and then provides practical ways to utilize each part of the workshop in an ELA or literacy classroom to maximize time, promote inquiry, and personalize learning for students.

Defining the Workshop Framework

Secondary teachers can borrow ideas from their elementary colleagues on how to best organize literacy learning. One method is to use a readers and writers workshop approach. Donald H. Graves (1983), whose seminal work birthed the writer's workshop prioritizing the writing process and placing an emphasis on student interest and choice, was influential in rethinking the structure of secondary ELA classes. The routine for the workshop includes: (1) beginning class with students engaging in a minilesson, (2) moving to independent writing during which teachers may conduct student conferences or pull small groups for intentional writing instruction, and (3) finishing the class period with sharing and celebration.

While acknowledging well-researched issues with the balanced literacy approaches espoused by Lucy Calkins (Goldstein, 2022; Wexler, 2021), her approach to reading and writing workshops with Teachers College Reading and Writing Project (n.d.) still offers valuable insights, noting these workshops "are deliberately designed to offer a simple and predictable environment so that the teacher can focus on the complex work of observing students' progress and teaching into their needs." To successfully implement an inquiry approach to learning, students and educators need a predictable learning structure.

While some may resist this idea of structure, as it seems to contradict the unstructured nature often associated with inquiry, the workshop framework actually opens up more time for choice, freedom, and personalized learning. Calkins and the TCRWP (n.d.) define five parts to the workshop framework:

1. Each session begins with a **minilesson**. Kids sit with a long-term partner while in the minilesson.

2. The minilesson ends with the kids being sent off to their own **independent work**.

3. As students work, the teacher confers with them and leads **small groups**.

4. Partway through independent work time, the teacher stands and delivers a **mid-workshop teaching point**.

5. The workshop ends with a **share**.

For the secondary classroom, break up the class period into three parts: (1) start together as a large group, (2) give students time to work independently in small groups or with you, and (3) end in a large group with a brief time together to share out the day's learning. Throughout each of the three parts of the workshop, a variety of intentional instruction and learning occurs.

1. **Start together (fifteen minutes):** The teacher and students engage in whole-group instruction in the form of minilessons, interactive read aloud, shared reading or writing, guided discussion, student-led instruction, and anchor chart creation.

2. **Engage in guided practice (twenty-five to thirty minutes):** Students work independently or in small groups to apply their learning and work toward mastery of braided learning goals. During this time, students might conference with the teacher, collaborate with peers, participate in station work, or read, write, or produce independently.

3. **End together (five to ten minutes):** The whole learning community comes back together to share out learning, generate areas of confusion or misconceptions, celebrate accomplishments, and provide valuable formative feedback to guide tomorrow's instruction and learning.

As you plan lessons with the workshop framework in mind, consider what students will be doing throughout the class period rather than what you will be doing (Tovani, 2011). Many ELA and literacy teachers find themselves with roughly a fifty-minute class period. For those on a block schedule where students are in class for ninety to one hundred minutes, consider running two workshops during the block.

Figure 4.1 provides a lesson-planning template you can use when designing literacy learning for secondary students in the workshop framework. (See page 141 for a blank reproducible version of this figure.)

Inquiry in ELA and Literacy Lesson-Plan Template Workshop Framework	
Inquiry Theme: Community	
Essential Questions: • How do we define community? • How can the individual positively impact the community? • How can the community serve individuals?	
Date: September 8	
START TOGETHER: Menu of Activities	
Text think-aloud/read-aloud options: • *The Curious Garden* by Peter Brown • *14 Cows for America* by Carmen Agra Deedy • *Chik Chak Shabbat* by Mara Rockliff • *The Name Jar* by Yangsook Choi • Current events articles showing communities in action **Minilesson topics:** • Defining *reading zone* • Managing distractions **Anchor chart prompts:** • Complete the fiction story structure outline with a picture book. • How are fiction and nonfiction structured differently? • What is stamina? Why is it necessary for maintaining focus while reading? • How do you manage distractions when trying to stay in your reading zone?	**Hour:** 1 English 9 **Learning goal(s):** I can manage distractions and remain in my "reading zone" for twenty minutes during class. **Activity:** Create an anchor chart for how to manage distractions while reading. Divide the chart into six parts: 1. What am I doing while I'm in my "reading zone"? 2. What am I *not* doing? 3. What is the teacher doing while I'm in my "reading zone"? 4. What is the teacher *not* doing? 5. What are my peers doing while I'm in my "reading zone"? 6. What are my peers *not* doing? Have students rehearse their ideas aloud with a partner. Then invite students to share in a large group. Record ideas (or invite a student to be the class writer) on chart paper.
GUIDED PRACTICE: Menu of Activities	
Conferring prompts: • What do you do to avoid distractions and ensure you understand what you are reading? • What does this book make you think about? • What in the text makes you think that? • What else are you wondering? • What do you want to know more about?	**Hour:** 1 English 9 **Learning goal(s):** I can manage distractions and remain in my "reading zone" for twenty minutes during class. **Activities:** Read for twenty minutes, and write about your reading in your reader-response journal for five minutes.

Collaboration activities:

- With a small group, complete a fiction story structure map with a picture book.

- Compare and contrast fiction and nonfiction texts for text structure.

Independent application:

- Read your independent reading book.

- Map the story structure of your independent reading book.

- Write about reading in your reader-response journal.

Conferring notes:

Record your notes on a conference template (see figure 4.2, page 121). Confer with your partner and discuss the engagement chart rating-scale (see figure 1.2, page 21). Confer with another classmate and see what they know about series books.

END TOGETHER: Menu of Activities

Share-out prompts:

- What is one discovery you made today?

- How would you rate yourself on the engagement scale for your independent reading?

Opportunities to make student work public:

- Students could choose a reader-response journal entry to share with a partner.

- Guided reading groups could share what they worked on and what they learned.

Exit-card prompts:

- What went well for you today? Where are you stuck?

- What are you reading? How do you like it so far?

- What is distracting you, and how are you managing it so you can stay in your "reading zone"?

Presentation ideas:

- Students or small groups could share their fiction story structure maps.

- Students could give short book talks.

Hour: 1 English 9

Learning goal(s):

I can manage distractions and remain in my "reading zone" for twenty minutes during class.

Activities:

Tell students that sharing is a "no judgment" share, and ask them to share with classmates where they felt their engagement was on the class engagement chart rating scale (see figure 1.2, page 21), and why.

Explain that it is OK if their engagement wasn't at a 4 or a 5, and today, you will look for reflections on why they are where they are, and how they might continue to improve.

Figure 4.1: Inquiry in ELA and literacy lesson-plan in the workshop framework.

Unlike a traditional lesson plan, for which you might have a very specific agenda with predetermined activities, in a workshop model, it is important to have a menu of activities to choose from so you can be responsive to what students need on that specific day. The left column offers a menu of activities. It isn't an exhaustive list; instead, it is a reminder of some of the activities available from the unit map. The right column shows the actual lesson plan for the day. This is often blank or filled in (in pencil) until the planning period prior to class.

STORIES FROM THE FIELD

Prior to using the workshop framework in my classroom, I prided myself on developing creative lesson plans filled with activities to engage students in the novel we were currently reading. It might be a day of readers' theater for chapter 3 of John Steinbeck's (1937) *Of Mice and Men* or a character study using three different versions of a scene from William Shakespeare's (1597/2011) *Romeo and Juliet*. Some days, students worked in the library researching their oral history paper; and other days, students spent the entire hour drafting their paper. I recall using full-length movies of books and plays as a reward after a traditional multiple-choice, short-answer, and essay test. This gave me three solid days to grade tests.

The challenge with this structure was that often my planning was more about what I would do as the teacher and less about what students were doing to master learning goals. Yes, I thought of how to keep students engaged, but it wasn't necessarily with a focus on learning. More so, I wanted to avoid off-task behavior that naturally was abundant during those research days in the library.

Making the switch to a workshop framework gave me and my students a structure to follow. I could be intentional about the time we would spend together as a large group, what students would be doing during guided practice, and how I was going to collect information and hold students accountable for their learning at the end of class as they shared out. I started by simply taking my original plan and putting it into the workshop framework.

For example, on *Of Mice and Men* (Steinbeck, 1937) readers' theater day, we took an excerpt from chapter 3 and talked about what we noticed, wondered, and predicted. We paid special attention to the characters' dialogue and how the narrator set up the way characters would say their lines. During guided practice, students were in small groups with a script I created for chapter 3. I created the script to focus on dialogue more than the narration. Students used their twenty-five minutes to divvy up parts, practice saying the lines with proper expression, and consider how they might play with the use of stools to create levels and blocking. During share time, the last ten minutes, we each shared a discovery or challenge from guided practice and reflected on improvements to make for performances the next day.

The whole-group time, which I didn't do previously, gave students a shared understanding of the tone Steinbeck (1937) established in this chapter and the way the characters spoke to each other. Sharing at the end, which I also didn't do previously, gave me valuable information about students' understanding of the text and the role expression and fluency plays in the comprehension. On a research workday, students were much more motivated and engaged during guided practice when we started with a research-skill minilesson and ended with students sharing their inquiry highs and lows.

Over time, workshopping my lessons became very natural. I did find that keeping to the time limit was a challenge. If we were having a great whole-group discussion, it was hard to cut it off at fifteen minutes. If students were all reading independently or working productively during guided practice, I didn't want to stop them for sharing time. I learned that the beauty of the workshop is giving each phase its time. So, to solve this challenge, I got a timer clock that showed the countdown and put a student in charge. There was always at least one student who enjoyed being the class timekeeper. In some classes, this responsibility rotated.

Next, we will examine each part of this workshop framework in more detail: start together, guided practice, end together.

Start Together

When building a community of learners, you need to spend time together as a large group. The beginning of class provides an opportunity to set the tone for the day and ground everyone in shared learning. Tovani (2011) also suggests an opening activity for students—just the first couple of minutes of the class period—to draw them in, give them pause to set aside any distractions, and orient them to the learning goals for the day. These openings might be a journal entry, a prompt on a nearby white board where students can respond, or an entrance ticket with a prompt students respond to and hand in for teacher review. This activity respects the learner in recognizing that they have had several classes, co-curricular activities, work, relationship interactions, and more that has taken place since you met previously. It also values the time needed to orient to and zone in on the day's learning goals.

After this opening activity, it is time for a whole-group shared learning activity. Even in high school, it can be beneficial to have students circle up, just like elementary students. Students should be sitting in a circle, even if, due to space constraints, it must be two circles (an inner one and an outer one), so they are all on an even level. Everyone is in the front row, so to speak. When the instructor joins the circle, ideally at the same level as the students, it reduces the visible power structure that can naturally occur between students and teacher.

The following sections explore in more detail how you can use text think-alouds, minilessons, and anchor charts in a short amount of whole-class instruction time at the beginning of the workshop to set the intention for the rest of the class period.

THINK ALOUD WITH A SHARED TEXT

Beginning the class period as a whole group thinking together around a shared text creates common experiences that build community, background knowledge, and shared understanding. You don't need to over-plan or overthink these opportunities. You simply need to curate a menu of short texts that will help you and your students, as a community, interrogate the unit's essential question and focus in on the learning goals. Picture books are an effective choice for a short text because they are quality texts with the added bonus of illustrations, which allow for access to the conversation for all learners.

For example, if you have students in class who are new to learning English, they can still engage in the thinking, even if it is in their first language in their head or on paper while seeing the story through illustrations. While you don't want to preclude yourself from using grade-level or above-grade-level texts during these text think alouds, be very intentional about your purpose. If your purpose is to get students thinking, consider that texts at a difficulty level of frustration will simply shut down thinking. If your purpose is to show strategies for navigating difficult text together, then a text with a high level of complexity is appropriate.

Other short texts that work well for a fifteen-minute, start-together discussion include poetry, song lyrics, excerpts from TED Talks or films, short films, photographs, articles, news clips, charts or graphs, statistics, policies, novel excerpts, essays, satirical cartoons, and so much more. If you are wondering if the text will work, simply consider if it will generate lively conversation. And always have a couple of backups ready if one flops.

Conducting a discussion with up to forty adolescents in a secondary classroom can be challenging. When you commit to using the workshop framework, you should help students explicitly understand how this learning structure operates. Students will want to know the *why* behind the structure as well as how it works and what is expected of them in each part of the class period.

One way to begin is to teach a minilesson on effective large-group discussion and set some norms as a learning community. Students can help generate characteristics of quality discussions and record these ideas on an *anchor chart*, which has information related to a particular task that can help students be successful. (See Create Anchor Charts, page 119, for more about anchor charts.) It can be a list of steps in a process, a set of vocabulary words related to the current topic, or anything else that has been discussed and students might need. You can create an anchor chart on a large sheet of poster paper and hang it in the room where it is easily visible to students. However, you can also use a Google Doc or Word document and pull it up on the large screen in the classroom or give students access on their individual devices, if available.

As you create the anchor chart with characteristics of a healthy and productive large-group discussion, prompt students with questions such as the following.

- How do we draw out students who are introverted?

- If we have a lot of ideas, how do we keep from dominating the discussion?

- What role do side conversations play (positive or negative)?

- When we disagree, how might we do so respectfully? What are some phrases we can use to show we value varied perspectives?

- How should we handle a situation in which someone says something sensitive or offensive?

- How might we stack on each other's thinking to move the discussion forward?

- What might we say or do when topics that seem irrelevant or tangential are brought into the conversation?

Consider having students do some writing and reflecting around these prompts ahead of a discussion and anchor chart creation or as follow up, so all students' voices are heard.

Table 4.1 (page 118) lists some challenges and ways to overcome them after norms have been established to keep the whole-group discussion moving forward successfully.

Table 4.1: Overcoming Whole-Group Text Think-Aloud Challenges

Challenge	Suggestion for Overcoming Challenge
Some students are dominating the discussion.	Give each student two tokens to use for contributing to the discussion. When they have used both tokens, they can write down any additional ideas they may have to be shared later.
Some students are participating in side conversations.	If side conversations seem to pop up with more than just an isolated pair or two, give the class time to turn and talk. Even if they are talking about something unrelated, it will give them a chance to get it out of their heads, so they can focus on the discussion.
Introverted students are not sharing.	During guided practice conferences, let introverted students know you'll be looking for nonverbal cues that they are thinking and have something to share (such as a furrowed brow or looking up and to the side). When you notice this, say, "I can see you are thinking; tell us what you are thinking or wondering." If the student responds that they aren't prepared to share, let them know you will come back to them after a couple more students share. Be intentional about returning to the student, so they know their voices and thoughts are valued.
Students are talking over one another.	Pause and have students write a thought on a sticky note. Ask them to pass the notes to their left. Keep passing until students have thoughts from peers across the circle from them. Then randomly call on students to share the thought on their sticky note. The original author does not have to get credit for the thinking.
Students are disagreeing disrespectfully.	Stop and refer to an anchor chart with phrases for disagreeing respectfully, such as: • I have a different perspective . . . • I wonder if we've considered . . . • I think the text is saying something different than what _____ just offered. Then invite students to start again with their thoughts.

OFFER MINILESSONS

Turning again to elementary colleagues who have spent more time teaching in a reader's and writer's workshop framework, secondary teachers can glean advice for how to organize minilessons. Minilessons are focused, short, direct, explicit teaching points. Often the educator connects that day's minilesson to the previous day's learning, explicitly teaches toward a learning goal, gradually releases to students so they can apply the learning, and then restates the explicit teaching point. These teaching points might be a comprehension strategy, community norms, research skills, conventions, aspects of the writing process, elements of genre and form, text features, author's purpose, and more. It is important to note that during minilessons, the teacher is teaching. This is a time when teachers are being explicit, direct, and concise in order to bring new learning to the community.

Minilessons should be reserved for teaching points that are new to the majority of the class. You don't need to spend time having students discover the rules for an APA citation, for example. You can teach it in a minilesson and then let students apply their learning during guided practice. It's also important to assess what students already know before moving to a minilesson. For example, if most students already have a thorough understanding of rhetorical devices used to persuade, you could reserve a minilesson for new learning, such as fallacy, if preassessment shows students don't yet fully understand this concept.

Rather than deciding ahead of time the sequence of minilessons, create a menu of topics from which to choose. This allows for more responsive teaching. If you are so rigidly planned, you may not be open to seeing what students already know and what they are ready to learn next. Another benefit of having a menu of activities is that you can make different decisions for various classes. Traditionally, if a secondary teacher is teaching the same ELA class and grade, the lesson plans from hour to hour will look identical. The students each hour are different, but the activities planned are often exactly the same.

With a workshop framework, you can see variations with the minilesson or text think aloud. Teachers may choose to use a picture book for the read aloud in one class, but the next hour, they may choose to do a minilesson instead because the students in that class indicated that is what they needed. The workshop framework allows for flexibility. You see more variety in the activities students do during guided practice, and the information students share at the end will likely look different from class to class.

CREATE ANCHOR CHARTS

Learning for Justice (n.d.a) defines an *anchor chart* as "an artifact of classroom learning. Like an anchor, it holds students' and teachers' thoughts, ideas, and processes in place. Anchor charts can be displayed as reminders of prior learning and built upon over multiple lessons." Often used in elementary classrooms, anchor charts can be beneficial for secondary students as well. When using anchor charts in secondary classrooms, it is important to remember to create them *with* students. You might be tempted to make one, laminate it, and use it in future school years.

However, Kristi Moore (2018) reminds educators that *the learning happens during construction*. Students need to own the thinking and then have immediate access to the ideas on an anchor chart posted prominently somewhere in the classroom. In other words, teachers should value the usefulness of the information over how attractive or creative it looks. Examples of how to use anchor charts in a secondary ELA classroom include the following.

- Information on how to cite sources using in-text citations following the appropriate or assigned style of formatting (for example, Modern Language Association [MLA], American Psychological Association [APA], or Chicago Manual of Style [CMS])

- Strategies for monitoring comprehension

- Norms for whole-group and small-group discussions, independent reading time, and listening

- Definitions and examples for rhetorical devices used in argument

- Delivery tips for formal speeches

When deciding how to use anchor charts, consider what tools will be helpful for students as they are practicing, producing, and performing. Students do not need to memorize everything, and tools like anchor charts can free up their working memory capacity as they develop long-term skills.

Guided Practice

Guided practice has been used in elementary settings to describe a process for implementing gradual release of responsibility, a strategy developed by P. Davide Pearson and Margaret C. Gallagher (1983)—the *I do, we do, you do* strategy. At the secondary level, Lyn Sharratt and Michael Fullan's (2013) definition of *guided practice* as a "transition practice that allows leaders to pull back and the learners to step forward" (p. 145) provides for more flexibility in its implementation.

In ELA and literacy classrooms, you can structure guided practice time (at least half of a class period) so students are getting the personalized practice they need. This can come in the form of high-level teacher support (conferences, teacher-led reading and writing groups, and one-on-one or one-to-few targeted explicit instruction), peer support (discussion and collaborative working groups), and low-level support (independent practice). Following are some ideas for guided practice with secondary ELA students.

HOLD TARGETED STUDENT CONFERENCES

You can accomplish so much by spending just five minutes or so in a one-on-one conference with a student. These intentional conferences can target one skill and often unlock the door to learning more than any fifteen-minute whole-class lecture can. Secondary ELA and literacy teachers can feel overwhelmed by the thought of conducting one-on-one sessions because they see 150 or more students each day. Even if you are only able to do one-on-one sessions with each student once or twice per term, the investment is worth the time.

To experience the benefits of conferencing, you need tools and a predictable structure for each conference. Figure 4.2 provides a template you can use on a clipboard or a tablet as a guide for the conversation and a place to keep notes. (See page 144 for a blank reproducible version of this figure.)

Name: Jorge G.

Hour: One

Teaching Points or Learning Goals:
Jorge is getting easily distracted while he reads and hasn't been able to maintain his stamina for the twenty minutes of independent reading each day in class.

Strengths:
Jorge is reading and comprehending his book *Black Boy White School* and can talk to me enthusiastically about it.

Opportunities for Growth:
Jorge confessed that he stays up late playing video games, so he is sleepy and more distracted during reading class. Finding ways for Jorge to discover how getting more sleep is beneficial might motivate him to turn the game off sooner.

Name: Aimee P.

Hour: One

Teaching Points or Learning Goals:
Aimee will be finishing the first *Cirque du Freak* book, and there are many books in the series. This is an opportunity to ask her what she knows about series and teach why they are engaging. This will be useful in helping her develop as a reader. I hope she is enjoying this one, so she can experience the fast pace one can read through a series once started.

Strengths:
Aimee was quick to find a book that captured her attention. It will be fun to see how she branches out from this series.

Opportunities for Growth:
Aimee still needs to grow in her ability to remove herself from distracting peers and manage the distractions that interrupt her ability to stay in her reading zone. Ask her what is working for her in this area, and see if she can set a goal to do more of what helps her. Focus on that, not the behaviors that get in the way (unless she brings them up).

Figure 4.2: Student conference template.

STORIES FROM THE FIELD

When I first set out to do reading conferences with my sophomores, I kept my focus very tight. I would conference with students about their independent reading books and get to know them as readers, using the conference to notice and name how they demonstrated their roles as readers and scholars. I admit that I didn't know what I was doing, and I didn't have a very strong system. Sometimes I didn't even bring a notepad with me. But that didn't diminish the benefits that came from the conferences. In the beginning, I would just kneel next to a student reading and prompt them to tell me about their book, why they chose it, if they liked it, and so on. These conversations helped students know that I cared about them, not only as readers but as humans.

They showed me so many assumptions I made about adolescent readers, both good and bad. And ultimately, these conversations deepened my relationships with students. Over time, I found it difficult to remember with whom I had conferenced and details about students' strengths and areas of need. So I realized I really needed a way to keep track of my notes. Using the student conference template on my clipboard (see figure 4.2, page 121) was helpful in keeping myself organized.

If you notice that more than one student needs support on a specific skill, hold a small-group conference or bring those students together for a guided reading or writing group. In addition to sticking to a structure, using an organizational tool, and keeping the conference short, Jennifer Serravallo (2019) reminds teachers, "Teachable moments abound in every moment of the teaching day, and conference time is no exception." She cautions, though, to teach one thing (Serravallo, 2019). Even if you see other areas of need, resist the temptation to go there, as it may distract you from the initial intention you set for the conference. Instead, make a note for a future conference, minilesson, or small-group instruction opportunity.

OFFER SMALL-GROUP INSTRUCTION

Guided reading and writing groups are commonplace in elementary schools, but at the secondary level, educators can underestimate the power of working with students in small groups. When you provide focused minilessons in small groups, it targets instruction in a personalized way for students who need it in that specific moment. We probably all have experiences when we were taught something, but by the time we were ready to apply it, we didn't remember what had been taught.

To help personalize learning for students in a targeted way, consider offering minilessons in small groups in a variety of ways. After noticing a concept that has been misunderstood or misapplied, offer a minilesson at a small-group table for anyone who would like to participate in guided practice. You also can develop pre-recorded minilessons that small groups of students can watch and collaborate on while you are working with another group. You may also invite students to teach minilessons if they have specific learning goals mastered.

The structure for these minilessons does not need to be complicated. At the secondary level, it often can feel overwhelming to think about planning for multiple small groups because planning daily lesson plans for five or six classes each day is so time consuming. Consider figure 4.3 (page 124) as a basic guiding structure for a small-group minilesson. (See page 145 for a blank reproducible version of this figure.)

Use the notes section to record your observations regarding students' strengths and areas in need of improvement. It is unlikely you will remember what happened in each small-group session, so having notes will jog your memory and help you set an intention for the next time you pull this small group or place an individual from the group with a new set of students.

Whenever possible, invite students to participate in small groups rather than assigning or requiring it. This builds adolescent autonomy, leans into the research behind adolescent engagement, and ensures student buy-in and participation in the small-group learning (Guthrie & Klouda, 2014). However, you may see students whose formative assessment tells you they really need the targeted instruction choose not to take advantage of small-group time when it is voluntary. When this happens, it provides an authentic opportunity for a one-on-one conference and coaching for that student.

Steps for Small-Group Instruction	Notes
1. **Introduce the concept or learning goal to the small group.** Today's concept for this group is thinking critically about what they read. They are using the text *Ants Work Together* by Nora Ellison. 2. **Ask students what they know about the concept or learning goal. Listen for both correct understandings and misconceptions.** Ask students what it means to think critically. 3. **Teach the concept or model the skill. If there is a specific writing or reading comprehension skill, consider having a mentor text handy.** Have a copy of *Ants Work Together* for each student, and ask students to open their reader-response journals to the list of critical-reading prompts (see figure 2.1, page 45). Read aloud and stop periodically to ask student to respond to one of the prompts. 4. **Ask students to try practicing the skill, and welcome their questions.** Ask students to think about the prompt: *When the author did . . . it helped me . . .* Continue with a discussion about nonfiction text features and how they help the reader. 5. **Notice and name the growth and progress toward mastering the learning goal.** I will be looking for higher-level thinking and pointing it out as I hear it. 6. **Take notes on further misconceptions that you can address in a one-on-one conference.** I will be listening for surface-level thinking and misconceptions and noting those.	**Student Name:** Mohammed **Notes:** Mohammed was attentive during the read aloud. He followed along in his book. The prompt he chose to answer was "It is clear the author wants us to know what we can learn from ants about how to work together." **Student Name:** Jenna **Notes:** Jenna was excited about the text we were reading. Jenna had a misconception that to read critically meant to criticize the reading. I will use this information to plan for our reading conference on Friday. **Student Name:** Martina **Notes:** Martina at first was not excited to read about ants because she thinks they are gross. But she immediately got pulled in to the photos, captions, and comparisons to humans. "10 quadrillion ants compared to 7 billion people?! Wow that is a lot!" She was intrigued by the numbers spelled out "10,000,000,000,000,000 versus 7,000,000,000" and wanted to share it with her math teacher. **Student Name:** No fourth student today. **Notes:**

Figure 4.3: Small-group instruction guide.

COLLABORATE IN GROUPS

While group work has its benefits, it also can be problematic. It can result in distributing work unevenly, furthering misconceptions, and promoting off-task behaviors.

Yet, if you heed the advice from a meta-analysis of 122 studies, you understand that you must provide opportunities for effective collaborative groups, as the effects are far greater than individual work or conditions that foster competition (Gillies, 2016). Jennifer Gonzales (2020) summarizes the key ideas of Gillies's (2016) meta-analysis:

> To be effective, cooperative work needs to be structured so that it embodies five key components:
>
> 1. **Positive interdependence:** Group members must work together to achieve a common goal.
>
> 2. **Individual accountability:** Each member is responsible for doing their part.
>
> 3. **Promotive interaction:** Group members help, support, and encourage each other.
>
> 4. **Effective interpersonal skills:** Students are taught how to communicate, solve problems, and resolve conflict effectively.
>
> 5. **Group processing:** Groups are given time to reflect on how well their group functioned and to make plans for improvement.

Fortunately for ELA teachers, many of the principles for cooperative learning also appear in our state ELA academic standards. We are expected to teach and create conditions for students to practice productive collaboration. As you develop inquiry units of study, be sure to balance guided practice time with opportunities for students to work in groups. Students can be in discussion or collaborative work groups to apply minilessons, workshop each other's writing, discuss shared texts, showcase learning, and teach one another. When engaging in a several-week-long inquiry unit of study, consider the following recommendations to avoid the common collaborative pitfalls with adolescents.

1. Keep groups to three or four students. Plan to keep the groups the same for the entire unit. You can create new groups for new units.

2. Be willing to make small changes in group makeup if necessary for groups to be productive.

3. Survey students ahead of time to determine strengths and preferences for working in groups. Be sure to balance strengths and personality types.

4. Consider the benefits and drawbacks for homogeneous versus heterogeneous groups. It can be advantageous to have homogeneous groups for book clubs in which students are all reading at a similar level.

When doing research, heterogeneous groups, related to students' literacy proficiency, can be helpful, as students will pursue inquiry questions and not necessarily reading the same texts. Each will bring strengths to the learning.

5. Explicitly teach collaboration skills. Use role play, read-alouds, video clips, and humor to showcase the enablers and barriers to productive group work.

6. Survey students during group work and find opportunities to course correct through minilessons and conferences.

7. Teach students how to manage conflict productively.

8. Celebrate when groups work through conflicts in a healthy way.

9. Conduct team-building activities and give groups small, manageable tasks prior to asking them to take on big projects.

You can't expect students to succeed by just putting them in groups. You must intentionally teach and coach students as they learn to be collaborative. This invest-ment made early in the year will pay off throughout all units of study and, more importantly, for students as they head out into careers or college.

PROVIDE HANDS-ON LEARNING OPPORTUNITIES

ELA teachers can embrace hands-on learning and resist the notion that this type of learning is reserved for science, career and technical education, or world language classes. Many learners in ELA classes don't see themselves as English students. Perhaps the student is proficient in auto mechanics, graphic design, gaming, or child develop-ment, and we are unaware of those strengths. If we bring in more of a maker mindset, one in which students empathize, ideate, and prototype solutions (Simmons, 2022), we will likely see skills and talents students can apply to their ELA work. After all, the same design thinking process you might use to prototype a design solution for a marketing project or create a new level in a video game is the same process you use to design a piece of writing. And when reading, you can gain greater understanding of the text and author's intent when you take a hands-on approach to comprehension.

Consider the idea of *novel engineering* (Novel Engineering, 2018), which focuses on students pondering a problem that a character in a book is experiencing and then ideating solutions. The hands-on part comes in when students create a prototype of their solution and test to see if it might work to fix the character's problem.

In her blog, *Using Picture Books to Engage Students in STEM/STEAM*, Lindsay Simmons (2021) shares the example of a picture book called *Penguin Problems* (2016), and how she asked young people to design solutions for one of the many problems the pessimistic penguin has, such as how his beak isn't cold enough or he isn't buoyant. After following the design process, Simmons (2021) says, "We shared our creations. We tested completed prototypes. We discussed our thinking. We asked questions. We talked about what we learned, and what we were still curious about." This process deepens student comprehension and can grow confidence for ELA students.

ENCOURAGE INDEPENDENT PRACTICE

Helping students become independent learners and thinkers is a goal all of us, as educators, have for our students. We want students to be able to manage their own distractions, pursue individual curiosities, and construct knowledge on their own. We don't want them to rely on their teacher or group members for all their learning. This is why balancing guided practice with teacher-led instruction, collaborative group work, and independent practice is critical.

In her *Edutopia* article, "Even Older Kids Should Have Time to Read in Class," Sarah Gonser (2021) states:

> If we want students to read—perhaps even grow to love reading—time for in-class reading needs to be prioritized in the school day. Far from being a waste of time, and in spite of intense pressures on teachers to meet academic requirements, when schools make the shift to incorporate in-class reading time, it can have a powerful, long-term impact on students' reading and writing skills.

Having students increase their volume of reading and writing is by far the best use of independent practice time. You can support students' comprehension and writing skills during this independent practice time. You also can help students notice and name distractions and coach them in ways to manage them so they can maintain engagement.

End Together

When the workshop framework is implemented well, the time can fly by. Students will be working so productively in groups or in such a complete state of flow with their independent work that it may be tempting to just let them work up until the bell. Don't do it. The five to ten minutes spent back together at the end of class is a critical component of the workshop framework. You can use this time to hold each other accountable for the day's learning as well as gather important formative assessment data to guide your adjustments for the next day's lesson plan. You don't need to overthink or overplan this sharing time. It's better to have a menu of activities and be flexible so you can respond to students in the moment. Some ideas for sharing include the following.

- Exit cards
- Sticky notes on which students share burning questions
- Whip-around share of discoveries made that day
- Brainstorming
- Anchor chart
- Think-pair-share
- Student sharing of writing
- Book talk

Throughout the workshop, create opportunities for students' voices to be heard every day. This can be the whole group, within teams, in a conference with a teacher, or by putting pen to paper and writing down ideas.

Figure 4.4 shows an example lesson plan utilizing the workshop framework—a day inside an inquiry unit on the essential question, *How can art and literature affect social change?*

Example Inquiry in ELA and Literacy Lesson Plan Workshop Framework
Inquiry Theme: Social change
Essential Question: How can art and literature affect social change?
Today's Date: October 10
Start Together (fifteen minutes)

Text Think-Aloud Options:	Learning Goals:
• Exhibits from "Art and Activism" The Art Institute of Chicago • "The 25 Most Influential Works of American Protest Art Since World War II" from *The New York Times Style Magazine* (La Force, Lescaze, Hass, & Miller, 2020) • *Because* by Mo Willems (2019) • *The Name Jar* by Yangsook Choi (2013) • *Those Shoes* by Maribeth Boelts (2009) • *Sometimes People March* by Tessa Allen (2020)	• Cite the textual evidence and make relevant connections that most strongly support an analysis of what the text says explicitly as well as inferences drawn from the text (CCSS.ELA-LITERACY.RL.9–10.1). • Learn about other people's histories and lived experiences and ask questions respectfully, listen carefully and nonjudgmentally (DI.9–12.8).

Minilesson Topics:

- Definitions for *social change, social inequalities*
- Social, political, and historical context for social justice issues
- Comprehension strategies
- Text or form features
- Author's purpose

Anchor Chart Ideas:

- Text feature observations
- Questions around social justice issues
- Ideas for further inquiry
- Strategies for monitoring comprehension
- Ideas for effective collaboration and authentic discussion

Activity:

Opening (five minutes):

- In your journal, describe how your book-club book relates to the essential question *How can art and literature affect social change?*

Read aloud (ten minutes):

- Share images from the "25 Most Influential Works of American Protest Art Since World War II" from *The New York Times Style Magazine* (La Force et al., 2020)
- Ask students in large group: "What do you notice?" "What are you wondering?" "What in this photo makes you think that?" "What do you want to know more about?"

Guided Practice (twenty-five minutes)

Conferring Prompts:

For Reading:

- What does this book make you think about?
- What do you do to avoid distractions and ensure you understand what you are reading?
- What in the text makes you think that?
- What else are you wondering?
- What do you want to know more about?

For Discussion or Collaboration:

- What role do you find yourself playing in your group book discussions?
- How is your preparation work going for small-group discussion?
- A learning goal I'd like you to keep in mind and reflect on is . . .
- What would you like to see work better for your discussion group?

Collaboration Activities:

- Further inquiry for book-club essential question
- Practice book discussion
- Creating art or literature to affect change in areas of interest to the students

Learning Goals:

- Prepare for and participate effectively in a range of conversations and collaborations with diverse partners (CCSS.ELA-LITERACY.SL.9–10.1).
- Maintain stamina for actively reading, managing distractions, and monitoring comprehension independently for twenty minutes.

Activities:

- Two book-club groups are in practice discussion.
- Four book-club groups are reading independently and preparing for book-club discussions coming up this week.

Conferring Notes:

- Meet with Abby to check on her comprehension of the book-club book. It's possible this book is a challenge, and she may need some additional scaffolds to help her independently access it.
- Check in with Donte to see if the audio book with the written text is working for him.
- Hold a comprehension conference with Ja'nae.

Figure 4.4: Inquiry in ELA and literacy lesson-plan example.

continued →

Book-Club Options:

- *Ghost Boys* by Jewell Parker Rhodes (2018) Essential question: What are the factors that create an imbalance of power within a culture?

- *You're Welcome, Universe* by Whitney Gardner (2017) Essential question: Can breaking the law or rules ever be justified?

- *The 57 Bus* by Dashka Slater (2017) Essential question: How are prejudice and bias created? How do we overcome them?

- *Drowned City* by Don Brown (2015) Essential question: What is the role of government to support and protect its citizens?

- *The Voting Booth* by Brandy Colbert (2020) Essential question: Who should have the power to elect leaders and change laws?

Independent Application:

- Create art or literature to affect change in areas of passion

- Self-reflection book-club discussion

- Reader-response journal for book-club book

- Further inquiry for book-club essential question

- Observe each of the practice discussion groups for five minutes, and provide notes on learning goals observed and those not yet observed.

End Together (ten minutes)

Share Out or Exit Card Prompts:

- How has your thinking changed from today's learning?

- What question is lingering in your mind as we close today?

- How might your collaborative team work together better?

- What topic are you hoping to learn more about?

Opportunities to Make Student Work Public:

- One book-club group models a short discussion about what they have read so far, while the rest of the class observes which learning goals are being demonstrated.

Presentation Ideas:

- Student share art or literature created to affect social change.

Learning Goals:

- Reflect on the day's learning, owning growth and areas of need.

Activities:

- *Whip share:* Each student shares their answer to this question: *How has your thinking changed today?*

Source for standards: National Governors Association Center for Best Practices & Council of Chief State School Officers, 2010.

project encouraging each other to shine. The illustrations shift from dull sketches to vibrant colors as the students come into their own confidence.

- *Ish* by Peter H. Reynolds (2004): Ramon loves to draw. Anytime. Anything. Anywhere. But when his older brother laughs at his art, Ramon loses confidence, crumpling up many drawings and tossing them into the trash. When Ramon discovers his crumpled drawings on his sister's walls, a new confidence is unleashed.

- *The Most Magnificent Thing* by Ashley Spires (2014): This charming book is about an unnamed inventor and her assistant, a dog, who set out to create the most magnificent thing. The inventor goes through many trials, frustrations, and discouragements. Her dog, suggesting a walk, helps her discover how reflection can lead to renewed enthusiasm and ultimate success. While she fails many times during the process, in the end when she accepts less than perfection, she sees how she did in fact make the most magnificent thing.

- *The Name Jar* by Yangsook Choi (2013): Unhei moves from Korea to the United States. When her classmates have trouble pronouncing her name, they all provide ideas on what her new American name could be by placing suggestions in a jar. On the day of her name choosing, the jar disappears, leaving Unhei with an important decision to make—keep her given name or find the jar so she can choose an American name.

- *Pink and Say* by Patricia Polacco (2003): This is a Civil War story passed down from great-grandfather to grandmother to son to author Palacco (2003). Say Curtis meets Pinkus Aylee, a Black soldier, and both are captured by Southern troops. This story celebrates the shared humanity between these rich characters.

- *Red: A Crayon's Story* by Michael Hall (2018): A crayon known as Red is feeling discouraged. No matter how hard he tries, he isn't able to successfully draw anything red. Many crayons in his life try to help him with no success. When Purple asks Red to draw a nice ocean for his boat, Red insists he can't, but Purple insists he can. What ensues is an identity shift for Red.

- *Those Shoes* by Maribeth Boelts (2009): Jeremy wants the popular new black high-top shoes everyone is wearing. His grandmother can't afford them. When Jeremy finds them for sale at a thrift shop nearby, he buys them even though they do not fit.

- ***Thunder Boy Jr.* by Sherman Alexie (2016):** Thunder Boy is named after his father, whose nickname is *Big Thunder*, rendering Thunder Boy to *Little Thunder*. He's not happy about it. He wants a name that embodies who he really is, so he brainstorms new names like *Old Toys Are Awesome*. But none seem quite right. His dad then helps him find a perfect name.

- ***What Do You do With a Problem?* by Kobi Yamada (2016):** A young boy has a problem that just won't stop following him. And the more the boy worries about it or avoids it, the bigger it gets. When the boy finally finds the courage to face the problem, he learns his greatest lesson.

- ***Zero* by Kathryn Otoshi (2010):** Zero is depressed. She doesn't see herself as having any value. She feels her life literally means nothing— zero. But with the help of her number friends, Zero quickly learns that she does have a purpose, and, through teamwork, she can add exponential value to others.

Start the class period by coming together in a circle and sitting on the floor, if possible. This can be tricky as students get older and bigger. Depending on the furniture in your classroom, students could place their desks in a circle as well. The circle is a symbol of community, putting each individual in the front row, able to make eye contact with one another and including the instructor as an equal participant.

When using a picture book for a read aloud, heed Peter H. Johnston's (2004) advice to invite thinking into the room but not judge it. He reminds us that when teachers don't evaluate, avoiding phrases like *good job*, it demonstrates that the focus is on the process of thinking, not the value of the thought (Johnston, 2004). As you read, stop periodically to ask open-ended questions such as, "What are you thinking?" "What are you wondering?" "What in the text makes you think or say that?" When students offer responses, instead of saying "Good" or "That's right," you might follow up with "Who else has an observation?" In time, students will build on each other's thinking. "I agree with Anna, but I also notice . . ." or "I have a different perspective than Abdul."

This activity, especially using easy-to-access texts, works well for building community and inviting all learners into the discussion. Even students who have newly immigrated to the United States and are just learning English can participate when you use books with illustrations or bring in bilingual books that have parts of the text in the student's home language.

Guided Practice With Zone Reading

Building the stamina to sustain reading is an important skill to foster in your classroom. Learners who are engaged in digital activities are finding it harder to focus on print text (Jabr, 2013). You can support students by setting aside guided practice time (twenty minutes) within a workshop block for sustained independent reading. Coaching students to help them identify what distracts them, engages them, and sustains them to maintain focused independent reading is critical for developing life-long readers.

A primary goal during this first community unit of study is to get students into books they will enjoy reading each day and hopefully love so much they will steal time to read outside of class. During this first unit, spend some of your start-together time discussing what it looks and feels like to be in your reading zone. Discuss with learners how to manage distractions, find engaging books, settle into a comfortable place in the room, and interact internally with the books they are reading.

Stories From the Field

During my first year teaching a reading course for striving learners, I took a whack-a-mole approach to getting students on task with reading. I would walk around the classroom and ask students to put their makeup and phones away and to stop throwing candy wrappers at classmates. Giving students suckers during reading time, thinking that would keep them quiet, was a misstep on my part. Fortunately, I learned early that this power struggle was not going to be successful, and coaching conversations would prove much more useful. I also learned that candy is not a motivator (Pink, 2011).

One student, Mia, was reading a book in verse and read each line as a sentence rather than reading to the punctuation. Once I helped her see how to read it, her comprehension (and enjoyment) of the book improved greatly. Another student, Jordan, seemed always to be sleepy in class, so I worked with him to brainstorm ways he could be more alert during the first hour so he could get in his reading

continued →

time. While I would have loved for Jordan to have an epiphany that playing video games late into the night was probably not helping him stay awake in the morning, we were able to discuss other ways he could be more alert (bringing a snack, sitting in a less comfortable seat). He took ownership for how he would get his reading minutes during our time together. I simply held him to the expectation we had agreed to as a class—twenty minutes daily for reading.

End Together

Finally, come back together in a circle for five to ten minutes to share. There are many ways students can share during this time. They can turn and talk with a neighbor about their zone scores. They can do a whip-around, in which students quickly go around the circle giving a brief answer to the question, "What book are you currently reading, and how many stars would you give it so far?" Or you could ask students, "How has your thinking changed today?"

Most important, aim to prioritize this part of the workshop framework. It's tempting to let students keep working if they are really maximizing their guided practice time. However, if you skip sharing, you miss the opportunity to gather important information to guide instruction for the next day. Sharing also shows students that you respect the learning they are doing during guided practice and want to hear about it.

STORIES FROM THE FIELD

As students walk into class midway through the community unit of study, I greet them while standing by the door. I tell them, "Look at the prompt on the white board. Use whatever color marker sings to you today to add a contribution to the board." On the white board, the prompt reads, "What are ways you show care to your family, friends, pets, or teammates?" Students respond with ideas such as:

- "I play fetch with my dog every day after school."

- "As captain, I am the first one ready to take the field but the last one to leave the locker room, so I can fist bump everyone on their way out."

- "I am trying to keep my room clean because otherwise my mom gets upset."

I enjoy coming into the room after the bell rings and watching a community of learners gather around each other at the board, reading what their classmates are writing and contributing their own ideas. A buzz of conversation gets the energy moving in a positive direction. The room is arranged in zones. See figure 4.5 for a visual of the classroom setup.

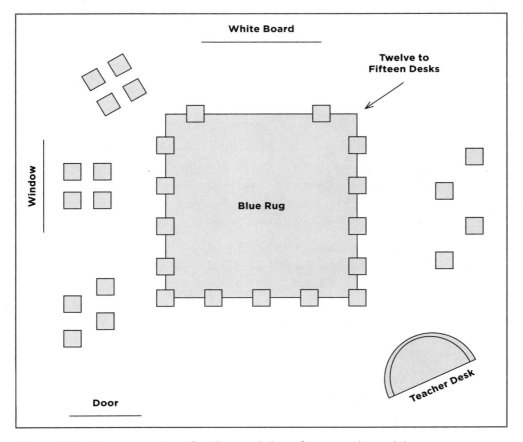

Figure 4.5: Classroom setup for the workshop-framework model.

continued →

We have a circle of fifteen desks around a blue rug in the front center of the space. Along the side wall and across the back are sets of desks arranged for collaboration for groups of four students. A couple of desks are set aside for independent work. This arrangement allows for the flexibility for whole group, guided practice, and independent learning.

Once students are in a circle, I present the book *The Curious Garden* by Peter Brown (2009), and let students know we are going to enjoy a story together as we continue to explore what it means to be in a community. Some students aren't yet buying in to the use of picture books in a high school class, but predictably, as I start to read, students quickly tune in—I can see they are enjoying being read to. The book is about a young boy who is out exploring one day in New York and discovers a garden growing in an unlikely place (Brown, 2009). The story is a great tool to have my community of learners explore inquiry, learning, and how one citizen's curiosity can positively affect an entire community. As I read, I stop periodically to ask one of three questions.

- "What are you wondering?'
- "What are you noticing?"
- "What are you thinking about?"

I may follow up with "What in the text or illustration makes you think that?" I don't worry too much about who is contributing or who is quietly engaging. If side conversations start to emerge, I will pause and ask students to talk to a partner about their thoughts so far with the book. This gives them an opportunity to be social with one another for a couple minutes and then I can re-engage students with the story. I spend just fifteen minutes on this activity and then stop. Ideally, I won't have finished the book. Why? Because it tends to motivate students to hurry back the next day so they can see what happens in the story.

At the end of this opening activity and interactive read aloud, I send students into guided practice time. They have two choices, which I have listed on the board.

Your choice:

1. Spend twenty minutes reading your independent reading book and then five minutes writing about your reading.

2. Grab a partner or two and a question from our inquiry jar to explore. Spend twenty minutes in the resource library and then five minutes writing about what you learned.

I have one primary goal—both options provide opportunities for students to achieve. The goal is for students to be authentically reading, writing, and thinking. The inquiry jar contains questions written on slips of paper that will help students explore the rich resource text set I have collected related to our theme of community, as well as a curated set of online resources (TED Talks, articles, infographics, news stories, and more). Students might draw a question such as *How does tragedy bring community together?* or *What are the characteristics of strong and weak communities?*

You might be worried about how distracting it might be for students who want to read their independent reading book to have partners reading and discussing what they are learning during the inquiry jar activity. Fortunately, we, as a class, have already established norms for noise level, respect, and managing distractions, so most students are able to find the right place in the room to engage in their choice activity.

After twenty-five minutes, there are now just five minutes before the bell. So that we end together, I ask students to write their name, class period, and either a question they have or something they learned today on a blank sticky note. They then hand me their notes on their way out the door.

I take a photo of the white board (too many good contributions to not keep a record), wipe it down for the next class, and take my spot at the door. While I wait for the new class to arrive, I browse students' sticky notes. Students' questions and learning help me decide if I need to adjust tomorrow's lesson. The activity also celebrates student learning.

Getting Started

Consider the following ideas as you intentionally structure the minutes of your ELA class period and embrace a workshop framework.

1. **Start by redesigning your current lesson plans in the start-together, guided-practice, end-together format:** Keep this up for at least a week. Ask students what they think. Reflect on how you are using the guided practice time. Be sure you use that time to interact with small groups or

one-on-one with students, and resist the urge to use it to lesson plan or take care of logistical items.

2. **Observe the workshop framework in action in a classroom:** Visit an elementary school or see if a colleague in your school uses it. Watching it in action can make it feel less intimidating.

3. **Interview students about their experiences with collaborative versus independent work:** Gather their feedback and work with students to come up with ideas to avoid the pitfalls. Recruit your classroom graphic designers or artists to make a visual anchor chart that you can display throughout the year as a visual reminder when group work gets challenging.

4. **Resist the urge to correct misconceptions in the moment:** Instead, prompt students with questions to direct their thinking or, if the misconception can linger until the next day, bring in new resources or texts that can push student thinking in a new direction. Encourage students to revise their thinking; remember, adolescents often resist being told they are wrong.

Conclusion

The workshop framework provides a rhythm and routine for the time we have with students each day. Starting together serves as a daily reminder that you are a community of readers, writers, and thinkers. It provides a time for whole-group, targeted instruction and an opportunity to engage in shared learning. You can use this time to model high levels of literacy, compile your thinking as a group, read and think about text together, and showcase student learning.

Guided practice allows for more personalized and responsive teaching and empowers you to coach students. If you want independent and collaborative learners, you must dedicate the bulk of your class period to students working alone or in small groups.

Ending together is a daily reminder to students that they are responsible for learning during class and sharing what they are learning with the community. During this valuable time, listen and observe, and gather the information you need to adjust the next day's lesson. The workshop framework is the structure needed to accomplish the goal of stepping aside and giving students control over their own learning.

Inquiry in ELA and Literacy
Lesson-Plan Template

Inquiry Theme: _____

Essential Questions: _____

_____

_____

Date: _____

START TOGETHER: Menu of Activities

Text aloud/read-aloud options:

_____

_____

_____

_____

_____

Minilesson topics:

_____

_____

_____

_____

_____

_____

Anchor chart prompts:

_____

_____

_____

_____

_____

_____

Hour: _____

Learning goal(s):

_____

_____

_____

_____

_____

_____

_____

Activity:

_____

_____

_____

_____

_____

_____

_____

page 1 of 3

GUIDED PRACTICE: Menu of Activities

Conferring prompts:

_____

_____

_____

_____

_____

_____

_____

_____

_____

Collaboration activities:

_____

_____

_____

_____

_____

_____

_____

_____

_____

Independent application:

_____

_____

_____

_____

_____

_____

_____

_____

Hour: _____

Learning goal(s):

_____

_____

_____

_____

_____

_____

_____

_____

Activities:

_____

_____

_____

_____

_____

_____

_____

_____

_____

Conferring notes:

_____

_____

_____

_____

_____

_____

_____

_____

END TOGETHER: Menu of Activities

Share-out prompts:

_____

_____

_____

_____

_____

_____

Opportunities to make student work public:

_____

_____

_____

_____

_____

_____

Exit-card prompts:

_____

_____

_____

_____

_____

Presentation ideas:

_____

_____

_____

_____

_____

Hour: _____

Learning goal(s):

_____

_____

_____

_____

_____

_____

_____

_____

_____

_____

_____

Activities:

_____

_____

_____

_____

_____

_____

_____

_____

_____

_____

_____

_____

Student Conference Template

Name: _____

Hour: _____

Teaching Points or Learning Goals:

_____

_____

_____

Strengths:

_____

_____

_____

Opportunities for Growth:

_____

_____

_____

Name: _____

Hour: _____

Teaching Points or Learning Goals:

_____

_____

_____

Strengths:

_____

_____

_____

Opportunities for Growth:

_____

_____

_____

Small-Group Instruction Guide

Steps for Small-Group Instruction	Notes
1. Introduce the concept or learning goal to the small group.	**Student Name:** _____ **Notes:** _____ _____
2. Ask students what they know about the concept or learning goal. Listen for both correct understandings and misconceptions.	_____ _____ **Student Name:** _____
3. Teach the concept or model the skill. If there is a specific writing or reading comprehension skill, consider having a mentor text handy.	**Notes:** _____ _____ _____
4. Ask students to try practicing the skill and welcome their questions.	**Student Name:** _____ **Notes:** _____ _____
5. Notice and name the growth and progress toward mastering the learning goal.	_____ _____ **Student Name:** _____
6. Take notes on further misconceptions that you can address in a one-on-one conference.	**Notes:** _____ _____ _____

CHAPTER 5

Creating Conditions for Student Engagement

When I first started teaching, I remember wanting to get positive evaluations from my administrator, especially on my classroom management techniques. I have always enjoyed order, structure, and minimal amounts of chaos. My classroom was neat, and I employed organizational processes so students would know where to find the agenda for the day, turn in homework, or pick up materials when absent. The desks were in neat rows, and I prided myself on keeping students on task for the full fifty minutes of English class. The marks on my evaluation for running an orderly and well-managed classroom were high. What I didn't realize in those early years was that just because students were on task, doing as they were instructed, didn't mean that students were engaged in authentic learning.

Teachers and students alike want to be in a class that is engaging, one where everyone looks forward to spending the time together. When you are intentional about creating conditions for student engagement, everyone benefits. When students are engaged, they persist through challenging tasks; they are comfortable wrestling with ideas and understand that frustration can be part of the learning process.

However, don't confuse engagement with excitement and energy, although those feelings can certainly work for an engaged classroom. Sometimes excitement and energy aren't necessarily related to learning. Considering who controls the learning is an important step in student engagement. Are students your puppets with them having the illusion of control, or do you truly let go so students can own their learning? When thinking about control in the classroom, you might think about your ability to manage students, keeping them "on task" and "under control."

The reality with adolescents, though, is that the more you try to *manage* them, which Merriam-Webster (n.d.b) defines as "to handle," "direct," or "to alter for a purpose," the more students resist. Similarly, don't confuse control with compliance. Students who are truly learning are in a productive struggle—persisting through challenge, as described in Supporting Students During Inquiry (chapter 4, page 109)—not shutting down because it is too hard or coasting because it is too easy. In engaged classrooms, students are in control. They are drivers of their own learning.

So, how do you create the fertile conditions for student engagement and control? You must create the atmosphere with teenage mindsets and behaviors in mind, commit to a regular routine and rhythm to the class period, foster relationships and rapport, be your students' coach, show students you want to know what they know and be responsive in your instruction, and assess learning in a supportive manner.

STORIES FROM THE FIELD

I was serving as a teacher on special assignment supporting middle and high school ELA teachers as they shifted paradigms and practices in ELA and reading to be more learner centered. Part of my role was to work alongside teachers in their classrooms as they reflected on current practice and considered changes.

I remember walking into a peer's classroom and immediately feeling at home. Her classroom was decorated beautifully—bulletin boards donned in mint green stripes and polka dots, and there were navy blue borders with pompoms made from yarn in each corner. Quotes in the most updated fonts adorned the walls. The teacher had organized bookshelves with books in woven baskets, displayed by theme, and nestled between trendy book ends. I noticed plants, reading corners with fun faux-fur pillows, shaggy rugs, and reading rockers (or gamer chairs)—also in navy blue and mint green. This was what I had dreamed my teenage bedroom could have looked like.

I thought, "I bet students love coming here!" So, I asked several students how they liked the classroom environment. In my unscientific and informal poll, I found students' reactions surprising. Many of them didn't have an opinion. Or I heard comments like, "It's so Ms. Howard," or "I am not a fan of polka dots." It struck me that none of the students felt like the classroom belonged to them. Most felt like they were walking into the teacher's space. I asked a few if they felt that way about other classes during their day. "Oh yes! Mr. Drummond is a huge Big Ten college sports fan and went to Nebraska—he has memorabilia all over his room," or "Mr. Short loves *Star Wars*, which I don't mind because I do too. He has so many Yoda posters, quotes, and figurines!"

One student described her science class in a very different way. She said, "I love my science classroom. When we first came to class, it was pretty bare. But over the first couple of weeks, our teacher began to organize the desks in the room in ways that worked for us, the students. She hung the posters we created about scientists we were studying and even took pictures of us doing labs and featured some of us in picture frames on her bookshelf."

As she talked, other students chimed in to agree, adding that they liked seeing the environment change and evolve as they moved through units and created more work. I didn't ever hear them describe the room as belonging to the teacher. They didn't come right out and say it, but I got the sense that they felt like the room was theirs. It gave me a whole new perspective on the role the physical environment plays in the classroom.

Structuring the Physical Environment

The physical environment is an important consideration for engaging adolescents in literacy. Of course, there are some aspects of the classroom that are in your control, such as how to arrange the desks, what to put on the walls, how to organize shared books and materials, and so on. Others are out of your control, such as the square footage of your classroom, the color of the walls (although it is possible to influence this), how many students are assigned to you, whether the classroom has a window for natural light and other similar variables. You may not even have your own classroom, as is often the case at the secondary level, which can limit your control. Following are some considerations for creating a physical environment that is engaging for adolescents, including furniture setup, décor, wall space, and reading nooks.

Furniture Setup

When setting up furniture in your classroom, consider that you will want space for large-group instruction, independent learning, small-group collaboration, and teacher-led small-group instruction. Ideally, you can set up the room so you don't have to move furniture during the class period, but sometimes that's not possible due to space limitations. In that case, you can train students to move desks (ideally on wheels) quickly to transition between components of the workshop framework (large-group minilesson, guided independent and small-group practice, large-group share).

Figure 5.1 shows a possible classroom setup. In this setup, when students are working or reading independently during guided practice, they could choose to sit at their table cluster or in the center of the room. Some may choose to find a place to sit on the floor at the perimeter of the room, leaning against a wall. Ultimately, flexibility for independent work is necessary so adolescents can remove themselves from distractions and focus on their work.

Décor

When decorating your classroom, create a warm and inviting space that feels homey but is neutral and not cluttered. Natural colors, plants (even if fake), baskets for books, bookshelves, and organizational bins for shared instructional supplies will help students feel welcome and relaxed for learning.

While it would be amazing if these decorations were provided for teachers, often they are not part of the budget because they aren't deemed essential. Securing donations, visiting thrift shops, or securing grant dollars can help accomplish the goal of creating a warm and inviting place for students to learn. Be careful as you are securing décor and items from donors or thrift stores that your environment doesn't end up looking like a mish-mash of items. For students to be engaged in learning, they need to have clear minds. When classrooms are full of clutter, stacks of papers, boxes, or students' clarity of mind suffers. Work toward organized, tidy, and clutter-free environments to ensure all brain capacity can be used for ELA and literacy learning.

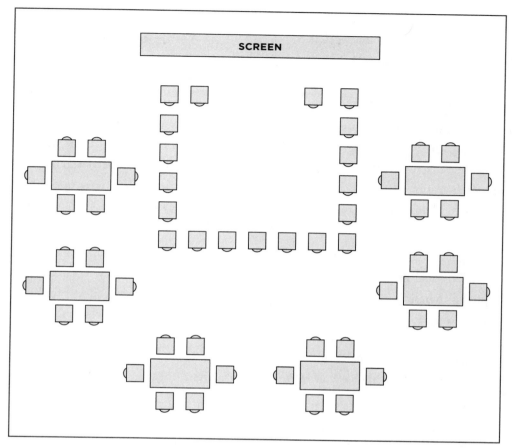

Figure 5.1: Possible classroom setup for workshop framework.

Wall Space

Students don't need inspirational, commercially created posters donning the walls. And while some commercial posters showing ELA content might be useful, students will engage more if they are part of creating these items. So go ahead and leave empty wall space for community-generated thinking on anchor charts or posters, student work for display (with their permission), and data displays.

A word about data displays: only showcase data that is worth celebrating and representative of the whole community, never an individual student—even if the data is anonymous. For example, set a goal for the term on how many books the class will read collectively. Then hang an empty chart where every time a student finishes a book, part of the chart is filled in. This shows the community how they are doing as they work together to accomplish their goal. Leaving a small portion of the wall space for personal items is important for showing students who you are and developing relationship and rapport. Remember that the classroom is a shared space; it's not just a place where students spend a short time during the day.

Reading Nooks

Create spaces that are cozy reading corners where students can curl up with a book during reading time. A rug, some pillows (with removable covers that can be washed), bookshelves to create division, and the illusion of isolation invite the reader to immerse themselves into a book. When students are in guided practice and have options for where they can choose to read or work independently, they are more likely to engage, manage their own distractions, and maintain stamina.

It can be hard to secure funding for these tools to support student engagement; however, local grants are a place to start. Sometimes you can make a case during capital purchasing (or whichever time your school allots for budget requests) for bookshelves especially. There is no one right answer for setting up the classroom environment, but whatever you can do to create the conditions for students to feel like the space is theirs, it is calm and comfortable, and the focus is student ownership of learning, not teacher delivery of information, the more engaged learners will be.

When students feel like the environment belongs to them, some of them may test the limits because this kind of environment feels unfamiliar. In the same way you meet students where they are with their learning, you can do the same with behaviors. Meet students where they are, and trust that with your coaching, they will eventually embrace independence, ownership, and community.

Students may take longer to focus on tasks or push back when asked to do something they don't think they enjoy, like reading and writing. Be patient and take notice when they do engage. In addition to the physical environment, if you want students to be independent learners, you have to intentionally create an environment to meet their social and emotional learning needs.

Structuring the Social-Emotional Learning Environment

The number of students reading for enjoyment continues to decline among nine-, thirteen-, and seventeen-year-olds, with boys consistently reading less than girls. In fact, "27% of juniors said they never or rarely read for fun on their own time"

(Schaeffer, 2021). The problem with students not reading for enjoyment is they are missing out on an activity that can help mitigate the rise in mental health challenges, especially anxiety and depression (Monroy-Fraustro et al., 2021). To increase the chances that students will begin reading for enjoyment, and in turn, reap the benefits, employ the following strategies: coach, engage student voice, confer, and showcase an inclusive collection of materials.

Coach

Students need an environment that feels safe emotionally (Sandler & Howell, n.d.). Students won't want to come to class if they fear they will be criticized instead of encouraged to grow. This could also affect their ability to build confidence. While most teachers do not set out to instill fear in students, many practices inadvertently do just that. When you walk around class redirecting students back on task, hand back assignments that point out all they are not doing well, and provide assessments that ask students to do something they haven't practiced and weren't aware was going to be on the test, this can be demoralizing and demotivating. You can shift to a coaching model by doing some of the following.

- Confer with students about their reading and support them in finding strategies to find the right book, manage distractions, and maintain stamina and attention while reading. This works better than noticing and naming off-task behaviors and asking students to stop. Sometimes the off-task behavior is a result of not having the strategies you can coach them to implement.

- Give students the opportunity to practice enough times before a summative assessment so they walk into the classroom knowing exactly what is expected and confident about how they will do. Using rubrics during the process can support this. For example, when students are having a book-club discussion as practice, have them use the same rubric you will use when you evaluate their discussions for a grade (see figure 3.8, Small-Group Book Discussion Rubric, page 89). They can use the rubric as a self-assessment or peer assessment, or you can listen in and give them formative feedback on the rubric. When students write papers, consider developing rubrics that show what they need to redo or revise, or how to identify if they are at a publishable place in their writing (Wiggins, 2022).

- Give students opportunities to redo assignments. How many times? As many as they need. This might sound uncomfortable, or you might fear that students will take advantage of you. However, when using rubrics and feedback (focusing on the learning, not the grade), students tend to do their best work first and are motivated to do better because they know the aim isn't points or a grade—it's to show what they know (Ferlazzo, 2021). Yes, you have to manage exceptions, but in these cases, you can move back into the coaching role and help students recognize their motivation for requesting a redo.

Engage Student Voice

When students feel like their voice matters in the classroom and that you will listen to them, it increases their agency. Teachers have such little time with students and so much instruction to do that it can be tempting to jump right into teaching. Choosing minilessons and content for direct instruction prior to gathering information from students on what they already know and can do can be an inefficient way to teach, not to mention disempowering for students. It can also be overwhelming to try to figure out baseline assessments to gather all the information you need to plan accordingly.

The good news is that simply by modifying the sequence of actions in the classroom, you can vastly improve your ability to be responsive. Instead of starting off a minilesson by teaching a concept, you can ask questions and draw out what students already know. You can offer an example of what you are trying to teach and ask students to observe and explain what they notice. For example, if the learning goal is for students to recognize the features of nonfiction texts and how they help the reader, instead of starting by directly teaching text features, you can provide an example of a page from an informational text and have students describe what they notice. By listening to students first, you can determine what they know, where they have misconceptions, and what they need to learn. You can then target upcoming minilessons, so they are much more responsive to what students need to know.

Confer

Another place where you can really listen to students is during one-on-one reading and writing conferences. When conferring with students, it can be tempting to prepare a lesson and do all the talking because you have so little time one on one. Instead, ask questions, listen intently, and observe how students are attending to the reading before providing a strategic lesson. Through one-on-one conversations with students, you build relationships and provide the most efficient and effective instruction.

Table 5.1 provides some simple prompts you can use when holding reading or writing conferences with students to get them to share their thinking.

Table 5.1: Prompts for Conferring With Readers and Writers

Prompts for Conferring With Readers
• What are you reading?
• Tell me a little about it (without spoiling the ending, of course!).
• Which character are you connecting with the most?
• Do any of your characters make choices you question?
• What about the [style, genre, topic] drew you to choose this book?
• Would you read another book by this author?
• Do you think I would like this book? Why? Why not?
• How do you manage distractions?
• How do you make sure you are understanding this book?
• What do you think you might read next?
Prompts for Conferring With Writers
• What are you drafting today?
• How is the writing going?
• Tell me about your process.
• Say more about that.
• What is tripping you up?
• What do you do when you get stuck?
• Would you consider trying _____?
• Is there a writer you admire or would like to emulate?
• Would it be helpful to see a mentor text?
• What do you need to do next?

Students need practice expressing their ideas in conversation. When you take the time to listen to them, encourage them to put their thinking into words, and collaborate with you, students are motivated to push themselves and grow.

Showcase an Inclusive Collection of Materials

Students feel accepted and welcomed in their classrooms when they see themselves in the materials you are using. In ELA, this means you must take a hard look at the novels you expect all students to read. If the characters or plot do not mirror your students, your purpose and intention for using the book should be very clear. Of course, you want to provide students with opportunities to have windows into others' experiences, but if students don't ever get a chance to see themselves, how are they going to engage?

Classroom book collections are a great way to ensure inclusivity. Inclusive class-room libraries ensure students' unique ethnicity, race, gender, language, socioeconomic status, religion, neurodiversity, physical abilities, and life experiences are represented (All-Access Classroom, 2021). In chapter 1 (page 13), I shared how I worked with Mackin's classroom department to create an initial library, and then worked with my students to organize and keep it fresh with new titles. It is important to include all kinds of books to meet the diverse needs and interests of students, including hi/lo books, fiction across all genres, nonfiction, poetry, graphic novels, books by authors who have authentic experience with what they write about (known as "own voices" authors), and more.

Turn to your librarian for help generating ideas for great books to have in your collection, advocate for capital funds to be spent on this essential tool for literacy in your classroom, and seek additional funding from community organizations who want to support literacy efforts in your school. Books students choose themselves from your classroom library work well for independent reading and book clubs.

As you consider the demographics and unique backgrounds of your students, you may want to reconsider the whole-class novels you choose for student reading. The required reading in schools is often the same as what students were required to read decades ago. Consider limiting whole-class novels and shifting to more individual-choice books. But when you do choose to have an anchor text, consider something more current and representative of the students in your classroom. Shift the stacks of classics to choices within book study units. Table 5.2 provides some alternatives for the most commonly read books at the secondary level. No contemporary substitution is perfect, but as educators, we need to challenge ourselves to consider what our purpose is in having all students read the same text, what our learning goals are for students, and how a more contemporary text might better serve to engage adolescents in reading and learning.

Sometimes bringing in contemporary texts can cause students (and some educa-tors) to feel uncomfortable. Sociologist Kia Heise provides a framework for navigating conversations around topics that some may deem as complex or controversial. She begins by asking that teachers reframe controversial topics as complex. Too often, teachers (and students) buy into the binary nature of topics and assume there are two sides to every issue. In reality, there are rarely two sides. When you zoom out and put a sociological lens to complex topics, which often surface when introducing contempo-rary titles to the ELA repertoire, you see nuances and multiple perspectives (K. Heise, personal communication, September 14, 2020).

Additionally, when you value questions over opinions, you invite students to consider multiple perspectives and resist the urge to provide "right" answers or under-developed ideas. One way Heise encourages educators to begin this work is by using picture books to launch inquiry when exploring social inequality themes or longer texts (K. Heise, personal communication, September 14, 2020).

Table 5.2: Classic and Contemporary Texts

Instead of or in Addition to This Classic Text . . .	Try This Contemporary Text	What It's About
The Outsiders by S. E. Hinton (1967)	*One Cut* by Eve Porinchak (2017) or *One of Us Is Lying* by Karen M. McManus (2017)	*One Cut* tells the true story of a group of friends whose involvement in a fist fight leads to a death. The prosecution paints the four defendants as gang members. The truth that comes out in the trial tells a different story. Porinchak weaves original sources, including court documents, trial transcripts, and interviews, throughout the book.
		One of Us Is Lying is about five students who have to attend after school detention at Bayview High. One of the five, Simon, is the creator behind the school's popular gossip app, and he is promising to spill the tea on each of the four co-detention attendees the following day. But, Simon doesn't make it out alive, and the four classmates all become suspects in his murder.
The Giver by Lois Lowry (1993)	*Alone* by Megan E. Freeman (2022)	In Freeman's multiple award-winning novel, *Alone*, twelve-year-old Maddie decides not to participate in a slumber party with her friends, and ends up waking up alone, left behind in a town that has suddenly become abandoned. Maddie is left to survive with her only companions being a dog named George, all the books she can read, and her stepbrother's book report on loneliness.
To Kill a Mockingbird by Harper Lee (1960)	*Sing, Unburied, Sing* by Jesmyn Ward (2017) or *Just Mercy* by Bryan Stevenson (2014)	In Ward's National Book Award-winning novel, *Sing, Unburied, Sing*, thirteen-year-old Jojo is trying to figure out what it means to be a man. This comes too soon due to his mom's addiction to meth, his siblings who need his care, and the fact that his father is in prison.
		Just Mercy tells how Stevenson founded the Equal Justice Initiative to help free falsely convicted inmates. Stevenson shares the case of Walter McMillian and others, showcasing ways people can improve the U.S. justice system to make it more fair and "merciful."

continued →

Nineteen Eighty-Four by George Orwell (1949)	*China Dream* by Ma Jian (2019)	*China Dream* is Ma Jian's satire of totalitarianism. In the story Ma Daode's life takes a nightmarish turn at the height of his career as the director of the China Dream Bureau. Jian's novel critiques the idea that the Communist party and its leader, Xi Jinping, can create a utopia in China.
Lord of the Flies by William Golding (1957)	*The Hunger Games* by Suzanne Collins (2008)	Set in North America, sometime in the future, *The Hunger Games* tells the story of an annual televised survival competition in which young people from each of twelve districts fight to the death, leaving one sole survivor. When sixteen-year-old Katniss Everdeen's sister Prim is chosen to represent their district, Katniss volunteers to take her place.
Romeo and Juliet by William Shakespeare (1597/2011)	*The Sun Is Also a Star* by Nicola Yoon (2016)	In *The Sun Is Also a Star*, Natasha, an undocumented immigrant from Jamaica, facing immediate deportation; and Daniel, struggling between what he wants and what his Korean family wants for him, have a chance encounter on the busy streets of New York City. Readers follow this star-crossed love story through alternating first-person narratives.
The Catcher in the Rye by J. D. Salinger (1951)	*Darius the Great Deserves Better* by Adib Khorram (2020)	In the award-winning *Darius the Great Deserves Better*, Darius' life is great. He is in a relationship, he and his dad are getting along, he stars on his high school soccer team, and he landed an internship. And then suddenly life is not so great. Darius starts questioning whether it is enough to just be OK, or if he deserves better.
The Grapes of Wrath by John Steinbeck (1939)	*American Dirt* by Jeanine Cummins (2020)	*American Dirt* is an extraordinary novel about the determination of Lydia, who must flee with her son Luca to protect him from the Mexican cartel. They face both danger and compassion on their quest for "American dirt."
The Great Gatsby by F. Scott Fitzgerald (1925)	*The Book of Unknown Americans* by Cristina Henriquez (2015)	In *The Book of Unknown Americans*, fifteen-year-old Maribel Rivera must leave behind her life in Mexico to receive medical care in the United States. While there, Maribel meets Mayor Toro, son of Panamanian immigrants, and they develop a romance. This is more than a love story. Henriquez weaves together a story illustrating the complexity of immigration.

When you consider creating a safe space for students in your classrooms, pay attention not only to the physical environment, but also to practices for the social and emotional environment that help students be seen and heard, ultimately feeling confident and welcome.

Getting Started

Consider these helpful ideas as you examine the conditions you create in your classroom for student engagement.

1. **Let students help you arrange and decorate your classroom:** Seek their input and help them problem-solve challenges with spacing and portions of the room that are immobile. Ask students to help organize book displays and choose what can be displayed on the walls.

2. **Ask students to help you keep a wish list of books to add to the classroom library:** Make this a living document that you keep and add to digitally, so when you are able to enhance or add to the classroom book collection, you have a list ready to go. Try using social media to garner support for fulfilling the list.

3. **Be flexible in physically setting up your classroom:** If what you thought might work for a group of students really doesn't, be willing to rearrange.

4. **Take action shots of students reading, writing, and collaborating:** Print photographs and put them in frames around the room. Change out photographs periodically. Students build confidence when they see themselves acting as scholars.

Conclusion

When you create the physical classroom environment in a way that is aesthetically pleasing, comfortable, free of clutter, and reflective of the students who will be in that space, meaningful learning can occur (O'Brien, 2023). You can solicit input from students on the physical arrangement of furniture, the décor that will don the walls, as well as how to organize the classroom library which will lead to student ownership and engagement in the space.

Equally, if not more, important is the social-emotional environment. Students need to feel safe, represented, welcomed, and respected when they walk into the classroom if advanced literacy learning is to occur (O'Brien, 2023). Ensuring the books students have to choose from include topics, characters, and plot lines that mirror their own lives or serve to expand their interests is necessary to encourage the love of reading. You might have to let go of the notion that the classroom belongs to the teacher, or the school, and instead be reminded that these spaces belong to learners.

CHAPTER 6

Celebrating Literacy Achievements

At the end of our first year implementing the Academic Literacy class, my colleagues and I knew we needed to celebrate the accomplishments our readers had achieved. Students had accomplished not only higher standardized test scores and academic achievement in other classes, but also the increased confidence and joy that comes with reading for fun (Plucker, 2010).

So, we invited students and their families to come to an awards ceremony and celebration in our school library on an evening in June before school ended. To incentivize students to come back to school in the evening, we told them there would be food, prizes, and surprises. We also asked them to invite a mentor. We asked that the RSVPs come to us so we could encourage students who were on the fence with messages such as, "Hey Max, your football coach said he was coming to our awards ceremony. You'll be there too, right?" We also offered childcare by having students from our National Honor Society and Early Childhood classes volunteer for service hours. We gave out awards to each student, handed out books and other prizes donated by our local community, and shared memories from our year together.

As students left, we encouraged them to keep reading over the summer by handing them an invitation for a midsummer BBQ where they could come check out more books, talk about what they were reading, eat, and socialize. Remarkably, about half of our students made it a priority to come to the BBQ.

When people achieve goals, finish projects, or accomplish a challenging task, they often find ways to celebrate. They might gather friends together for a celebratory meal or reward themselves with a recreational outing. Or they might receive a tangible object to commemorate the achievement—a medal after a marathon or a certificate with a seal and signature authenticating it.

In school settings, sometimes these celebrations are reserved only for co-curricular activities or a culmination of academic achievements for some, but not all students, such as the National Honor Society and academic honor rolls. These are important ways to celebrate and should be preserved, but how might you ensure that *all* students have the opportunity to celebrate their accomplishments and growth in ELA? Celebrating student success in the classroom enhances student engagement, memory, and achievement, and ultimately makes them feel good about themselves (Smith, n.d.).

As you consider how to celebrate students' achievements, consider the role of rewards in the learning process. Rewards don't have to necessarily be tangible. Intangible rewards, such as achieving a goal, reflecting on hard work, and sharing success stories, are all ways you can celebrate.

Offering Rewards

Before getting into some practical ways to celebrate in ELA, be cautious of what you consider as rewards for students. In some cases, rewards can be harmful to student motivation (Pink, 2011). Educators often use external rewards (for example, grades, stickers, points, praise) to motivate students to do the work. The problem with this is the activity can focus on the reward instead of the actual learning. Findings from a 2016 Student Gallop Poll shows the steady decline in student engagement after fifth grade, with tenth, eleventh, and twelfth graders reporting being disengaged or actively disengaged far more frequently than engaged (as cited in Calderon & Yu, 2017). For students to remain engaged in the classroom, appeal to their intrinsic motivation. *Intrinsic motivation* is fostered by offering students choice, building their confidence, and focusing on the process more than the product (Anderson, 2021). Some ways to promote intrinsic motivation include the following.

- Always give students some choice when assigning reading. If they aren't able to choose the book, can they choose to read it in print, large print, or digital?

- Increase the complexity of the texts students are reading to build confidence. For example, if a student hasn't successfully read an entire book from front to back in a while, consider suggesting an easier book—a hi-lo book, a book in verse, or a graphic novel. Once the student finishes the book successfully, the next book can be a little harder.

- Help students see value in the process of wrestling with difficult text. You can do this by modeling your own struggle with a challenging passage. Students can see what you, as an accomplished reader, do when you get stuck reading.

Setting Goals

When students set their own goals, they are more intimately connected to the learning (Anderson, 2021). You can help students set learning goals by writing them in student-friendly language, providing examples, and coaching students toward goals that are in their proximal zone, or sweet spot, of learning. When it comes to *grading* goals, ultimately it is best for goals to be formative and used as a tool for learning. However, depending on the culture of grades in your learning community, you may find it helpful to give students points for setting goals and reflecting on their progress toward achieving the goals. Ideally, when students accomplish a goal, it will translate to successfully demonstrating learning on a summative assessment.

When students set their own learning goals, it is less important that they have the precise steps for achieving them, and more important that they go through the exercise of thinking about how they might achieve those goals and how it is going along the way. The act of setting and reflecting on goals increases student ownership in the learning, regardless of whether you think their steps for getting there are correct or not (Rankin & Casey, 2022). For example, if a student sets out to manage distractions so they can achieve the goal of maintaining independent reading stamina for twenty minutes, and one of the steps for achieving that goal is to ask a distracting peer to not be in class the next day, you might not agree with that idea. The exercise itself is what is most important for achieving the goal.

Figure 6.1 (page 164) provides a template that students can use to record how they will set, reflect on, and achieve learning goals. This figure shows an example of how a student might complete the template. Consider filling in the learning target or goal for students or completing that information together. (See page 173 for a blank reproducible version of this figure.)

Setting, Reflecting on, and Achieving Learning Goals

Unit: Literature and Social Change

Essential Questions:

- How can literature promote social change?
- How can policies that seem fair result in unfair treatment?

Learning Target or Goal	My Steps for Achieving the Goal	My Reflection Date: October 21	Did I achieve the goal? If not, why not yet?
I can self-select a book for independent reading.	1. I will browse books related to the essential question. 2. I will read the first page and ensure I can understand what I am reading. 3. From the books that I feel I can read independently, I will choose at least two that are interesting and provide that information to my teacher.	I got one of my two choices and am about one-third of the way through the book. I am not having much trouble comprehending the text, and it is holding my interest so far. I feel like this goal is obtainable.	Yes, I finished my book and understood it well while I was reading it.
I can manage distractions and remain in my "reading zone" for twenty minutes during class.	1. I will find a comfortable spot in the room away from friends who can distract me. 2. I will leave my phone at my desk or in my bag and not bring it with me while I am reading. 3. I will use the strategy of re-reading if I find my mind wandering.	The first few days were hard. I kept wanting to check my phone, wondering if I was missing notifications. But I was proud of myself for not having my phone with me and finding a quiet spot away from friends who might distract me. After the first few days, I found it was much easier to get in my zone, partly because the plot picked up in my book, and partly because I realized the notifications can wait.	I eventually met my goal of maintaining attention for twenty minutes each day, but it did take me a while to get there, and some days I still struggle with finding myself thinking about other things and having no idea what I just read. I think this might be a goal I will continually have to work on.

| I can synthesize perspectives and cite evidence from my text set to answer essential questions. | 1. I will record my thinking in my reader-response journal after reading each day and be sure to include some quotes and page numbers to support my ideas.
2. When given other texts to read, I will take notes on the printed article or infographic, so I have my thinking annotated for later synthesis.
3. I will listen and record ideas from my book club on their thoughts related to our book and text set.
4. I will keep track of my questions.
5. I will track perspectives as I read and keep notes related to which text provided insight on each perspective. | Ooof! This goal is hard. I am learning that my note taking is not very organized. I thought I would set up a document with columns for each perspective on the essential question, but I found that determining specific perspectives was hard.

One of my group members had a great idea of using colored sticky notes related to different ideas and perspectives our group was discussing. I am going to try that idea this week. | I think my goal was too lofty. I was able to cite text evidence when providing ideas related to the essential question. The evidence of this is in my reader's notebook and some of the assignments we did in class.

I am not sure I have a good grasp on synthesizing the many perspectives related to the question yet. I'm glad we will have more opportunities to practice synthesizing. |

Figure 6.1: Setting, reflecting on, and achieving learning goals template example.

Continually prioritizing learning goals for students and asking students to map out their learning journey and reflect on what is going well and what needs to change not only motivates them but also proves successful for student mastery of learning (Rankin & Casey, 2022). Reflecting and making new goals builds confidence and promotes mastery with completion and compliance (Anderson, 2021).

STORIES FROM THE FIELD

For many years while teaching, I was also the head coach of a large high school speech and debate team. At the state, local, and national levels, our program was recognized as premier. When you have more than one hundred students competing, there will always be some students on the team who do not take home trophies each week, while others qualify for the regional, state, or national competition. For all students on the team, but especially those who did not get public accolades, it was critically important to offer other ways of recognizing achievement for both the short term and long term.

To accomplish this, we did several things. We had students set goals and reflect on them. We informally recognized wins we would see in judges' comments on their critiques from the previous week's competition. Our captains introduced awards to be given each week at team meetings that were related to qualities outside of competitive success, such as team spirit, dedication, growth, and motivation.

Because our team was highly ranked and we competed against other teams who were also highly ranked, the competition was fierce. Therefore, we had to ensure students participating in this activity didn't feel their value came from winning nor that the value they were getting from the activity was measured in trophies. Students needed to realize that the skills they were developing throughout the process—poise, confidence, charisma, nonverbal skills, and more—were the true rewards of the activity. We knew these skills would benefit students in life way more than any medal or trophy might. When we set goals, we helped students keep their focus on the messages they were crafting and the skills they were learning, not the results that might not be in their control.

So, a goal might look like this: "My goal for my humorous interpretation is to develop each of my characters distinctly, each with their own comedic attributes and timing," instead of "My goal is to win the state competition in humorous interpretation." We noticed that when we made this shift, students took much more ownership of their process and internalized it rather than looking for external reasons for both failure and success.

Celebrating Short-Term Wins

Celebrating short-term wins can build momentum and help students maintain engagement in learning. You can reward the short-term wins in ELA classrooms in a variety of ways, such as the following.

- **Pats on the back:** In this activity, students have the opportunity to partner up and ask peers how they are doing on their goals. Then they can provide a public "pat on the back" by sharing with the learning community something positive they heard their peer share about their progress. Teachers can also provide public "pats on the back" that come from formative assessments they reviewed or conferences they had with students.

- **Community goal chart:** On chart paper, draw a large outline of your school's mascot. In my case, we're the lightning, so I draw a large lightning bolt. Set a class community goal, such as number of books read in a quarter collectively by students in the class. Then, as students finish a book, they color in a bit of the mascot until it is filled in when the class goal is achieved. This emphasizes community over the individual and provides a visual representation of short-term progress toward a long-term goal.

- **Call or message home:** When you notice a short-term accomplishment, make an effort to send a message home recognizing that accomplishment. Be sure to outline the learning goal the student is working toward, so you are intentionally recognizing progress toward that long-term goal.

- **Photo booth:** Who doesn't love a photo booth at a party or wedding, one in which there are props, such as hats, mustaches, signs, and other items, to use when taking goofy photos. Ask students to work in small groups to generate ideas for how they might demonstrate their short-term achievements on a goal through photo-booth props. Give them popsicle sticks, paper, scissors, and access to computer graphics, and let them create. Remember, the process is more important than the product. Reflecting while having fun creating *is* the celebration.

The best way to foster students' short-term wins is through descriptive feedback on the formative assessments and through one-on-one or small-group conferencing (Ferlazzo, 2021). Whenever you can notice and name the effort students are putting into achieving learning goals and connecting that effort with results, you are celebrating short-term wins.

Celebrating Long-Term Wins

Be sure to celebrate long-term achievements as well, both individually and as a community of learners. Following are some ideas to inspire your celebrations.

- **Create reflection videos:** Have students create reflection videos sharing how they have grown as readers, writers, and thinkers. Be sure to require they provide some evidence of that growth for you.

- **Make a class song playlist:** Create a class playlist of songs that represents learning and growth throughout the year. Each student contributes one song (radio-appropriate version) and explanation for the playlist.

- **Showcase student work:** Showcase student work publicly in the classroom. You can physically hang student work on a wall or virtually make it available in your learning management system or using a website like padlet.com. Make an effort to showcase something from every student at least once during the term. It can be a summative assessment, like a full paper, or something small such as a memorable line from a piece of writing or performed speech.

- **Conduct award ceremonies:** These ceremonies can be at the end of units as well as a culminating activity at the end of the year. Have students nominate their peers for awards and ensure each student gets one. Ideally, the awards are linked to learning goals, such as "avid reader," "comedic writer," "charismatic speaker," and "quality collaborator."

Reflecting

The practice of reflection in education is often seen as either an event (such as having students reflect in preparation for student-led conferences) or as an afterthought (such as having students reflect on their grade on a paper after it is finished, published, and graded). Consider reflection as an ongoing daily practice, an important instructional tool for student learning and teaching. Ruth Heyler (2015) states:

> Reflection is more all-encompassing than just "looking back." People instinctively reflect on events, perhaps to better understand what has happened and make sense of it; the idea of learning from the past, especially trying not to repeat mistakes, is well established. (pp. 21–22)

This shift in thinking can also open your mind to all your instructional practices that can also serve as reflective tools.

Reader-Response Journals

Reader-response journals, introduced in chapter 1 (page 13), serve as a place for students to record their thinking while reading. Students also can reflect on their comprehension skills, ability to think critically about what they are reading, how they monitor their focus, and setting goals for improving their reading skills. The practice of recording thinking and having instructors read and respond to that thinking provides an opportunity for celebration as well.

Portfolios

ELA skills are recursive and compounding, meaning many of the learning targets you might be working on early in the year are going to resurface frequently. You might provide opportunities for students to approach a learning goal they may feel they have mastered with greater sophistication and more nuance. For example, if a student is able to cite evidence from text to support a claim, perhaps the next level would be to find two more pieces of evidence within the text to strengthen the argument.

Keeping a portfolio can be helpful for students to see their growth and work toward higher levels of application. Just like when we look back at photos and reminisce on memories from the past, so too can students reminisce on experiences in the classroom and how they have grown as readers, writers, and thinkers by reflecting on work samples in their portfolio.

While educators may want students to keep a digital portfolio since so much of what is created in ELA exists online, there is something powerful in having a tangible portfolio. Just like we enjoy having prints in a photo album, students also like having a printout of a paper or a photo of themselves participating in a lively discussion or giving a speech. Printing excerpts and including a QR code or short link to the full document can save paper, but you can still have a hard copy in the portfolio for students to page through.

Exit Cards

Exit cards, described previously in chapter 1 (page 13), provide an opportunity for students to give brief information to the teacher as they leave class. While many ideas exist for using exit cards, following are a couple that can work well either during the opening or sharing portions of your workshop.

- **What? So What? Now What?** First, students reflect on what they are currently learning or where they might be stuck. Next, students write about why it is important to identify what is halting their learning process. Finally, students develop a plan for getting unstuck, such as seeking support from a peer, setting up an appointment for a conference with the teacher, or revisiting the exemplars or instructions provided for the task.

- **Stoplight—Red, Yellow, Green:** Students reflect on what is stopping them from learning (red), what is slowing them down (yellow), and what is coming easily so far (green).

Storytelling

The art of storytelling has tremendous benefits in the classroom. Neurological research points to a release in oxytocin in the brain, that feel-good chemical that increases one's attention when watching or listening to stories (Foy, 2019). Stories help people learn and remember. Because storytelling can make us feel good, it is a natural choice for celebration. So, what does it look like to bring storytelling and celebration together in an English class? Consider some of the following ideas.

When the school year begins, celebrate the unique gifts each student brings to the learning community. You can do that through six-word memoirs, an idea generated by Larry Smith, founder and editor of *Smith* magazine (2021). In this activity, ask students to write something about themselves using only six words. Students could read short biographies of authors they will meet throughout the English course and consider how they are like and different from the author. When students share those comparisons and contrasts with the class, they not only are learning about their classmates but also about the authors they will meet through reading and writing during the school year.

Finally, it is important to tell stories at the end of the year as a way to culminate a year of learning together. Students can create a video of highlights from the year as a way to celebrate, and teachers can use those the next year to get students excited about what is to come. It is important to have students collect clips, artifacts, photos, quotes, and more throughout the year so they have them for compiling the culminating story at the end of the year. Keeping these artifacts in their physical and digital portfolios makes the project easier later in the year.

A few programs students can use for digital storytelling and portfolios include the following.

- Book Creator (bookcreator.com) is an online storytelling app. It is free to get started, but if you love it, you'll want to upgrade to the paid version.

- Picklits (picklits.com) is a free app that allows students to add text to images through freestyle writing or drag-and-drop.

- Powtoon (powtoon.com) in an app where students can create up to three-minute animated videos for free.

- Animoto (animoto.com) is an easy-to-use, free video creation software.

Getting Started

When celebrating students' literacy learning throughout the year, keep the following ideas in mind.

1. **Avoid including food in your celebrations:** First, some students have allergies. Second, food can easily become the reason students do the work—for the candy, donuts, or pizza—instead of for the learning. If you do decide to include food, make it a surprise so it doesn't serve as an incentive.

2. **Give students choice whenever possible:** When students are reflecting, give them at least two prompts or an option to skip a prompt on an exit card. Even managed choice motivates students to own their learning.

3. **Share stories outside the classroom:** Allow parents, administrators, the local education foundation, and more, to hear students' stories and

see their accomplishments. Students may resist this at first but will come to see that public recognition for authentic learning is really rewarding, probably even more so than pizza or candy.

4. **Wean students off points for reflection and goal setting:** When students own the learning, they can be demotivated by points that tend to serve as an incentive. This may take a little time, but try not putting grades in the gradebook for these celebratory activities and see what happens.

Conclusion

I wonder if sometimes educators feel like they can't take the time to celebrate because there is so much content to work through and standards for students to master. Yet, creating and following through on well-planned intentional celebration leads to more intrinsic motivation for students (Anderson, 2021). Celebration doesn't have to be a separate event, although it can be. Celebration can be ongoing throughout the learning process through goal setting, reflection, storytelling, and student choice.

Setting, Reflecting on, and Achieving Learning Goals

Unit:

Essential Question:

Learning Target or Goal	My Steps for Achieving the Goal	My Reflection Date: _____	Did I achieve the goal? If not, why not yet?

Epilogue

I set out to write this book in 2019. Authoring a professional book for peers was a brand-new endeavor. Although I was sometimes paralyzed by the thought that what I was writing might be outdated by the time this book hit the shelves, I continue to work alongside teams of teachers who are applying the principles and ideas outlined in this book—ideas my previous teammates and I were trying more than a decade ago. Teachers are energized. Their students are finding joy.

As I wrote this book, I will admit that some doubts crept in. I worried that people reading this book might think it was too simple or too straightforward. Did I need to be more innovative?

And yet, getting adolescents excited about and engaged in text really is quite simple. They need opportunities to read, write, talk, think, collaborate, and reflect every day. Students should be reading texts they are interested in, talking about ideas they care about, collaborating with one another to make sense of what they are learning, writing about their reading, writing to create or remix or emulate, and revisiting questions with new and fresh perspectives just to come back the next day to do more thinking while they read, write, and talk all over again.

Of course, I do not mean that teaching this way is easy. In the past, I have over-complicated the teaching of reading and ELA and forgotten to step aside, listen to my students, and let them do the driving so they can own their learning, which are all foundational principles of inquiry.

When you provide students with choice and opportunities for their voices to be heard and valued, you create a community of learners. Be intentional about the physical and social-emotional learning environments you create so students feel safe to take risks and struggle productively in their quest to become readers, writers, and communicators. When you immerse young people in rich experiences to explore a variety of texts—from picture books, trade books, contemporary novels, and nonfiction, to TED talks, articles, infographics, and more—you invite curiosity and opportunities for students to authentically wrestle with topics they genuinely care about.

To make this shift to inquiry, both teachers and students need structure. The workshop framework has been that rhythm and routine, opening the doors to student ownership and personalized learning in my and many other ELA classrooms. Intrinsic motivation plays a key role in students owning the learning process when you adopt the inquiry model. To foster student motivation, be sure students understand the purpose for reading, writing, and collaborating; ensure autonomy in the process; and be in constant pursuit of mastery (Pink, 2011). Finally, students will benefit from goal setting, reflection, and storytelling as celebration in the ELA classroom.

There are so many brilliant and innovative ideas out there, but don't forget that *you, too,* have ideas. Trust that what you bring to students every day is enough. Use the ideas presented in this book to affirm or inspire you to regroup, remix, or innovate in the name of adolescent literacy engagement.

My goal in writing this book is to remind educators of the essential and valuable role they play in convincing young people to become lifelong readers by providing time for them to read high-quality and engaging texts, giving choices for what they read, and creating optimal physical and psychological conditions for learning.

I thank all of you who share this goal and are committed to changing the lives of the students you teach through books.

References
and Resources

Adams, P. (2021, October 24). *The truth about inquiry-based learning.* Accessed at https://theage.com
.au/education/the-truth-about-inquiry-based-learning-20211012-p58z8v.html on April 17, 2023.

The Alexander Group. (2019, May 19). *2019 Commencement speeches call for community, kindness and critical thinking.* Accessed at https://tagsearch.com/insights/articles/2019-commencement-speeches
-call-for-community-kindness-and-critical-thinking on April 17, 2023.

Alexie, S. (2016). *Thunder Boy Jr.* (Y. Morales, Illus.). New York: Little, Brown.

All-Access Classroom. (2021) *How to build a culturally inclusive classroom library to embrace student diversity* [Blog post]. Accessed at https://theallaccessclassroom.com/how-to-build-a-culturally
-inclusive-classroom-library-to-embrace-student-diversity on April 17, 2023.

Allen, T. (2020). *Sometimes people march.* New York: HarperCollins.

Anderson, M. (2021). *Tackling the motivation crisis: How to activate student learning without behavior charts, pizza parties, or other hard-to-quit incentive systems.* Alexandria, VA: Association for Supervision and Curriculum Development.

Andres, M. (2018). *Community service and volunteering.* Ada, OK: PowerKids Press.

Atwell, N. (2007). *The reading zone: How to help kids become skilled, passionate, habitual, critical readers.* New York: Scholastic.

Banchi, H., & Bell, R. (2008). The many levels of inquiry. *Science and Children, 46*(2), 26–29.

Barbaro, M. (Host). (2021, October 11). *Which towns are worth saving?* [Audio podcast episode]. Accessed at https://nytimes.com/2021/10/11/podcasts/the-daily/climate-crisis-resilience.html on April 17, 2023.

Becker, A. (2014). *Journey.* London: Walker Books.

Blackburn, B. (2018). Productive struggle is a learner's sweet spot. *Productive Struggle for All, 14*(11). Accessed at www.ascd.org/el/articles/ productive-struggle-is-a-learners-sweet-spot on May 25, 2023.

Blythe, C. (2013). *Revenge of a not-so-pretty girl.* New York: Random House Children's Books.

Boelts, M. (2009). *Those shoes* (N. Z. Jones, Illus.). Somerville, MA: Candlewick Press.

Bowen, J. (2021, October 21). *Why is it important for students to feel a sense of belonging at school? 'Students choose to be in environments that make them feel a sense of fit,' says associate professor DeLeon Gray.* Accessed at https://ced.ncsu.edu/news/2021/10/21/why-is-it-important-for-students -to-feel-a-sense-of-belonging-at-school-students-choose-to-be-in-environments-that-make-them-feel -a-sense-of-fit-says-associate-professor-deleon-gra on July 5, 2023.

Braga, A. (2022, March 22). *The importance of children's representation in literature and media.* Accessed at www.humanium.org/en/the-importance-of-childrens-representation-in-literature-and-media on July 5, 2023.

Brown, D. (2015). *Drowned city: Hurricane Katrina and New Orleans.* Boston: Houghton Mifflin Harcourt Books for Young Readers.

Brown, P. (2009). *The curious garden.* New York: Little, Brown Books for Young Readers.

Burns, A. (2022, January 6). *Building trust with students—even before class starts: How to promote psychological safety in your classroom.* Accessed at https://hbsp.harvard.edu/inspiring-minds/building -trust-with-students-even-before-class-starts on July 5, 2023.

Bush, J. (2007). *Ana's story: A journey of hope.* New York: HarperCollins Publishers.

Calderon, V. J., & Yu, D. (2017, June 1). *Student enthusiasm falls as high school graduation nears.* Accessed at https://news.gallup.com/opinion/gallup/211631/student-enthusiasm-falls-high-school -graduation-nears.aspx on April 17, 2023.

Cali, D. (2016). *The truth about my unbelievable summer. . .* San Francisco, CA: Chronicle Books.

Cassidy, S. (2022). *The moon is a silver pond, the sun is a peach.* Victoria, BC, Canada: Orca Book Publishers.

CBS News Minnesota. (2021, October 25). *"It's more than the machinery": Farmers come together to help family in need.* Accessed at https://cbsnews.com/minnesota/news/karson-lindblad-dies-boyd-farmers -help/?utm_campaign=true_anthem&utm_medium=social&utm_source=facebook&fbclid =IwAR3aTmef54dBF-B3wwR5HMSX8ePya3jmI-D9Q7xqsqqbuBICIFcQr1e8bsI on April 17, 2023.

Centers for Disease Control and Prevention. (2022, March 23). *New CDC data illuminate youth mental health threats during the COVID-19 pandemic.* Accessed at www.cdc.gov/media/releases/2022/p0331 -youth-mental-health-covid-19.html on June 24, 2023.

Choi, Y. (2013). *The name jar.* Columbus, OH: Zaner-Bloser.

Chong, S. B. (2014). *Community gardens: Grow your own vegetables and herbs.* New York: Rosen Publishing Group.

Clinton-Lisell, V. (2019). Reading from paper compared to screens: A systematic review and meta-analysis. *Journal of Research in Reading, 42*(2), 288–325. https://doi.org/10.1111/1467-9817.12269

Colbert, B. (2020). *The voting booth* (M. Senders, Illus.). New York: Disney Hyperion Books.

Collier, E. (1994). *Breeder and other stories.* Baltimore: Black Classic Press.

Collins, S. (2008). *The Hunger Games.* New York: Scholastic Press.

Collins, S. (2010a). *Catching fire.* New York: Scholastic Press.

Collins, S. (2010b). *Mockingjay.* New York: Scholastic Press.

Common Sense Media (2014). *Children, teens, and reading* [Research brief]. Accessed at https://commonsensemedia.org/sites/default/files/research/report/csm-childrenteensandreading -2014_0_1.pdf on April 17, 2023.

Coombs, K. (2023). *Today I am a river.* Louisville, CO: Sounds True Publishing.

Cordell, M. (2016). *Hello! Hello!* New York: Disney Hyperion Books.

Cornelius-White, J. (2007). Learner-centered teacher-student relationships are effective: A meta-analysis. *Review of Educational Research, 77*(1), 113–143.

Coy, J. (2010). *Crackback.* New York: Scholastic.

Culley, B. (2020). *Three things I know are true.* New York: HarperTeen.

Cummins, J. (2020). *American dirt.* London: Tinder Press.

Daniels, H. (2017). *The curious classroom: 10 structures for teaching with student-directed inquiry.* Portsmouth, NH: Heinemann.

Davies, M. (2018). *You can too! Change the world.* Huntington Beach, CA: Teacher Created Materials.

Daywalt, D. (2015). *The day the crayons came home.* New York: Philomel Books.

Deedy, C. A. (2018). *14 cows for America* (T. Gonzalez, Illus.). Atlanta, GA: Peachtree.

Divecha, D. (2019, May 9). *Our teens are more stressed than ever: Why, and what can you do about it?* [Blog post]. Accessed at https://developmentalscience.com/blog/2019/5/7/our-teens-are-more-stressed-than-ever on April 17, 2023.

Drummond, A. (2011). *Energy island: How one community harnessed the wind and changed their world.* New York: Macmillan.

DuFour, R., DuFour, R., Eaker, R., Many, T., & Mattos, T. (2016). *Learning by doing: A handbook for Professional Learning Communities at Work (3rd ed.).* Bloomington, IN: Solution Tree Press.

Duke, N. K., Purcell-Gates, V., Hall, L. A., & Tower, C. (2006). Authentic literacy activities for developing comprehension and writing. *The Reading Teacher, 60*(4), 344–355. https://doi.org/10.1598/rt.60.4.4

Elhillo, S. (2021). *Home is not a country.* New York: Random House Children's Books.

Elley, W. (1991). Acquiring literacy in a second language: The effect of book-based programs. *Language Learning, 41,* 375–411.

Ellison, N. (2018). *Ants work together.* Ada, OK: PowerKids Press.

Farber, M. (2017, May 14). *5 genius hour tips.* Accessed at www.pbs.org/education/blog/5-genius-hour-tips on July 5, 2023.

Fenske, J. (2016). *Barnacle is bored.* New York: Scholastic.

Ferlazzo, L. (2021, March 5). *Grades should be a 'feedback tool.'* Accessed at www.edweek.org/teaching-learning/opinion-grades-should-be-a-feedback-tool/2019/11 on July 5, 2023.

Fitzgerald, F. S. (1925). *The great Gatsby.* New Delhi, India: Laxmi.

Fleischman, P. (2013). *Seedfolks* (J. Pedersen, Illus.). New York: HarperCollins.

Foy, G. M. (2019, September 8). *Are we the stories we tell?* [Blog post]. Accessed at https://psychologytoday.com/us/blog/shut-and-listen/201909/are-we-the-stories-we-tell on April 17, 2023.

Frankel, K. K., Becker, B. L. C., Rowe, M. W., & Pearson, P. D. (2016). From "what is reading?" to what is literacy? *Journal of Education, 196*(3), 7–17. https://doi.org/10.1177/002205741619600303

Freeman, D. (1964). *Dandelion.* New York: Puffin Books.

Freedman, R. (2009). *Freedom walkers: The story of the Montgomery bus boycott.* New York: Holiday House.

Freeman, M. E. (2022). *Alone.* New York: Aladdin Books.

Fullerton, A. (2023) *Community soup.* Toronto, Ontario, Canada: Pajama Press.

Galileo Educational Network. (2015, December 2). *What is inquiry?* [Blog post]. Accessed at www.galileo.org/blog/what-is-inquiry on April 18, 2023.

Gallagher, K. (2006). *Teaching adolescent writers.* Portland, ME: Stenhouse.

Gallagher, K. (2009). *Readicide: How schools are killing reading and what you can do about it.* Portland, ME: Stenhouse.

Gardner, W. (2017). *You're welcome, universe.* New York: Knopf.

Gillies, R. M. (2016). Cooperative learning: Review of research and practice. *The Australian Journal of Teacher Education, 41*(3), 39–54. https://doi.org/10.14221/ajte.2016v41n3.3

The Global Read Aloud. (n.d.). *The global read aloud: One book to connect the world.* Accessed at https://theglobalreadaloud.com on April 17, 2023.

Glover, M., & Keene, E. O. (Eds.). (2015). *The teacher you want to be: Essays about children, learning, and teaching.* Portsmouth, NH: Heinemann.

Goetz, S. (2018). *Old Macdonald had a boat.* San Francisco, CA: Chronicle Books.

Golding, W. (1957). *Lord of the flies.* London: Faber & Faber.

Goldstein, D. (2022). *In the fight over how to teach reading, this guru makes a major retreat.* Accessed at www.nytimes.com/2022/05/22/us/reading-teaching-curriculum-phonics.html on May 25, 2023.

Gonser, S. (2021, February 26). *Even older kids should have time to read in class.* Accessed at https://edutopia.org/article/even-older-kids-should-have-time-read-class on April 17, 2023.

Gonzales, J. (2020, February 3). *Making cooperative learning work better.* Accessed at https://www.cultofpedagogy.com/making-cooperative-learning-work-better on April 17, 2023.

Gonzalez, M. V. (2022). *Build strong communities.* Mankato, MN: Capstone Press Inc.

Gorman, A. (2021). *The hill we climb: An inaugural poem for the country.* New York: Penguin.

Graves, D. H. (1983). *Writing: Teachers and children at work.* Portsmouth, NH: Heinemann.

Green, E. L., & Goldstein, D. L. (2019, December 5). *Reading scores on national exam decline in half the states.* Accessed at https://nytimes.com/2019/10/30/us/reading-scores-national-exam.html on April 17, 2023.

Guthrie, J. T., & Klauda, S. L. (2014). Effects of classroom practices on reading comprehension, engagement, and motivations for adolescents. *Reading Research Quarterly, 49*(4), 387–416. https://doi.org/10.1002/rrq.81

Hall, M. (2018). *Red: A crayon's story.* New York: HarperCollins Children's Books.

Hansberry, L. (1959). *A raisin in the sun.* New York: Random House.

Harvey, S., & Daniels, H. (2015). *Comprehension and collaboration: Inquiry circles for curiosity, engagement, and understanding* (Rev. ed.). Portsmouth, NH: Heinemann.

Hasak-Lowy, T. (2022). *We are power: How nonviolent activism changes the world.* New York: Abrams Books for Young Readers.

Hattie, J. (2009). *Visible learning: A synthesis of 800 meta-analyses relating to achievement.* New York: Routledge.

Heise, K. (2022, May 3). *Complex books, in context series.* Accessed at https://mackinlearning.com /complex-books-in-context-series on April 17, 2023.

Henriquez, C. (2015). *The book of unknown Americans.* New York: Vintage Contemporaries.

Heyler, R. (2015), Learning through reflection: The critical role of reflection in work-based learning (WBL). *Journal of Work-Applied Management, 7*(1), 15–27.

Hinton, S. E. (1967). *The outsiders.* New York: Viking Press.

Hoffman, M. (2016). *Amazing grace* (C. Binch, Illus.; 25th anniversary ed.). New York: Dial Books for Young Readers.

Hughes, L. (2014). *Thank you, ma'am* (C. Molinari, Illus.). Parker, CO: Child's World.

Ivey, G., & Johnston, P. H. (2013). Engagement with young adult literature: Outcomes and processes. *Reading Research Quarterly, 48*(3), 255–275.

Jabr, F. (2013, April 11). *The reading brain in the digital age: The science of paper versus screens.* Accessed at https://scientificamerican.com/article/reading-paper-screens on April 17, 2023.

Jackson, S. (1948, June 19). *The lottery.* Accessed at https://newyorker.com/magazine/1948/06/26/the-lottery on April 17, 2023.

Jian, M. (2019). *China dream.* Berkeley, CA: Counterpoint.

John, J. (2016). *Penguin problems.* New York: Random House Books for Young Readers.

Johnston, P. H. (2004). *Choice words: How our language affects children's learning.* Portland, ME: Stenhouse.

Judge, L. (2019). *Flight school.* New York: Little Simon.

Kamkwamba, W., & Mealer, B. (2009). *The boy who harnessed the wind: Creating currents of electricity and hope.* New York: HarperCollins.

Kelley, M., & Clausen-Grace, N. (2013). *Comprehension shouldn't be silent: From strategy instruction to student independence* (2nd ed.). Newark, DE: International Reading.

Khorram, A. (2020). *Darius the great deserves better.* New York: Dial Books.

La Force, T., Lescaze, Z., Hass, N., & Miller, M. H. (2020, October 15). *The 25 most influential works of American protest art since World War II.* Accessed at https://nytimes.com/2020/10/15/t-magazine/most-influential-protest-art.html on April 17, 2023.

Lamatina, A. (2023). *Reading refresh: Strategies to reinspire good reading habits.* Accessed at https://mackinlearning.com/reading-refresh-strategies-to-reinspire-good-reading-habits on July 5, 2023.

Lamba, M., & Lamba, B. (2017). *Green: A community gardening story* (S. Sánchez, Illus.). New York: Farrar, Straus and Giroux.

Latson, D. (2017, June 7). *The power of community* [Video file]. TED Conferences. Accessed at https://ted.com/talks/dontae_latson_the_power_of_community/up-next on April 17, 2023.

Layne, S. L. (2009). *Igniting a passion for reading: Successful strategies for building lifetime readers.* Portland, ME: Stenhouse.

Learning for Justice. (n.d.a). *Anchor charts.* Accessed at https://learningforjustice.org/classroom-resources/teaching-strategies/exploring-texts-through-read-alouds/anchor-charts#:~:text=An%20anchor%20chart%20is%20an on April 17, 2023.

Learning for Justice. (n.d.b). *Social justice standards.* Accessed at https://learningforjustice.org/frameworks/social-justice-standards on April 17, 2023.

Lee, H. (1960). *To kill a mockingbird.* London: Longman.

Literacy Today. (2023). *Reading inquiry.* Accessed at www.literacytoday.ca/home/reading/reading-inquiry on April 17, 2023.

Lowry, L. (1993). *The giver.* New York: Houghton Mifflin Harcourt.

Lucy Calkins and Teachers College Reading and Writing Project (TCRWP). (n.d.). *The predictable 5-part workshop framework.* Accessed at www.unitsofstudy.com/framework on April 18, 2023.

Ludwig, T. (2013). *The invisible boy* (P. Barton, Illus.). New York: Knopf.

Luther, V. L. (2022) The impacts of self-efficacy and intrinsic motivation: Mentoring students to be motivated readers. *The Language and Literacy Spectrum, 32*(1), article 2. Accessed at https://digitalcommons.buffalostate.edu/lls/vol32/iss1/2 on July 5, 2023.

Mack, G. (2001). *Mind gym: An athlete's guide to inner excellence.* New York: McGraw Hill.

Mackin. (2021, December 1). *Resource development form.* Accessed at https://home.mackin.com/classroom/resource-development-form on July 5, 2023.

Maiers, A. (2012, January 30). *In Google we trust* [Blog post]. Accessed at https://edtechdigest.blog/2012/01/30/in-google-we-trust on April 17, 2023.

McCanna, T. (2017). *Watersong.* New York: Simon & Schuster.

McCombs, B. L., & Whisler, J. S. (1997). *The learner-centered classroom and school: Strategies for increasing student motivation and achievement.* San Francisco: Jossey-Bass.

McManus, K. M. (2017). *One of us is lying.* New York: Delacorte Press.

Merriam-Webster. (n.d.a). *Engage.* Accessed at https://merriam-webster.com/dictionary/engage on April 18, 2023.

Merriam-Webster. (n.d.b). *Manage.* Accessed at https://merriam-webster.com/dictionary/manage on April 17, 2023.

Meyer, S. (2005). *Twilight.* Boston: Little, Brown & Company.

Miller, D. (2008). *Teaching with intention: Defining beliefs, aligning practice, taking action, K–5.* Portland, ME: Stenhouse.

Minnesota Department of Education. (n.d.). *English language arts standards.* Accessed at https://education.mn.gov/mde/dse/stds/ela on July 5, 2023.

Mitchell, S. (2020). *All out: The no-longer secret stories of queer teens throughout the ages.* Toronto, Ontario, Canada: Inkyard Press.

Moje, E. B., Richetta, R. L., Santelises, S. B., & Steiner, D. M. (2017, February 17). *The adolescent literacy crisis in America* [Video file]. Accessed at https://edpolicy.education.jhu.edu/the-adolescent-literacy-crisis-in-america on April 17, 2023.

Monroy-Fraustro, D., Maldonado-Castellanos, I., Aboites-Molina, M., Rodríguez, S., Sueiras, P., Altamirano-Bustamante, N. F., de Hoyos-Bermea, A., & Altamirano-Bustamante, M. M. (2021). Bibliotherapy as a non-pharmaceutical intervention to enhance mental health in response to the COVID-19 pandemic: A mixed-methods systematic review and bioethical meta-analysis. *Frontiers in Public Health, 9,* 629872. https://doi.org/10.3389/fpubh.2021.629872

Moore, K. (2018, August 12). *Everything you need to know about using anchor charts.* Accessed at https://moore-english.com/using-anchor-charts-in-secondary on April 17, 2023.

Morse, J. C. (2012). *Scholastic book of world records, 2012.* New York: Scholastic.

National Governors Association Center for Best Practices & Council of Chief State School Officers. (2010). *Common Core State Standards for English language arts and literacy in history/social studies, science, and technical subjects.* Washington, DC: Authors. Accessed at www.corestandards.org/assets/CCSSI_ELA%20Standards.pdf on April 17, 2023.

The Nation's Report Card. (2023). *Scores decline again for 13-year-old students in reading and mathematics.* (2023). Accessed at www.nationsreportcard.gov/highlights/ltt/2023 on July 5, 2023.

Novel Engineering. (2018). *Homepage.* Accessed at https://novelengineering.org on April 17, 2023.

O'Brien, S. (2023, May 15). *A guide to the environment as the 'third teacher'* [Blog post]. Accessed at https://thespoke.earlychildhoodaustralia.org.au/a-guide-to-the-environment-as-the-third-teacher on July 5, 2023.

Olson, C. B., & Land, R. (2007). A cognitive strategies approach to reading and writing instruction for English language learners in secondary schools. *Research in the Teaching of English, 41*(3), 269–303.

Orwell, G. (1949). *Nineteen eighty-four.* London: Secker & Warburg.

Otoshi, K. (2010). *Zero.* Mill Valley, CA: KO Kids Books.

Pearson, P. D., & Gallagher, M. C. (1983). The instruction of reading comprehension. *Contemporary Educational Psychology, 8*(3), 317–344. https://doi.org/10.1016/0361-476x(83)90019-X

Pelzer, D. (1995). *A child called "it": One child's courage to survive.* Deerfield Beach, FL: Health Communications.

Pink, D. H. (2011). *Drive: The surprising truth about what motivates us.* New York: Riverhead Books.

Plucker, J. M. (2009). *From frustration to freedom: Intervention for striving readers.* Accessed at www.slideshare.net/jenniferplucker/from-frustration-to-freedom on May 22, 2023.

Plucker, J. M. (2010, October 1). *Baiting the reading hook.* Accessed at https://ascd.org/el/articles /baiting-the-reading-hook on April 17, 2023.

Plucker, J. M. (2022a). *Carrots and candy: Letting go of rewards in favor of true motivation.* Accessed at https://mackinlearning.com/carrots-and-candy-letting-go-of-rewards-in-favor-of-true-motivation on July 5, 2023.

Plucker, J. M. (2022b). *Inquiry in ELA: 10 ways to make it work.* Accessed at https://mackinlearning.com /inquiry-in-ela-10-ways-to-make-it-work on July 5, 2023.

Plucker, J. M. (2022c). *Prioritize helping our students fall in love with reading (again).* Accessed at https://mackinlearning.com/prioritize-helping-our-students-fall-in-love-with-reading-again on July 5, 2023.

Polacco, P. (2003). *Pink and say.* Pine Brook, NJ: Lectorum.

Porinchak, E. (2017). *One cut.* New York: Simon Pulse.

Rankin, B., & Casey, R. (2022). Goals, growth, and grades: Student ownership of learning through reflection. *NECTFL Review, 89,* 57–64.

Regional Educational Laboratory Program (REL). (2017, June 1). *What is the current research on sustained silent reading?* Accessed at https://ies.ed.gov/ncee/rel/Products/Region/central/Ask-A -REL/20033 on July 5, 2023.

Renaissance Learning. (2016). *What kids are reading: And how they grow.* Accessed at http://celi.olemiss .edu/wp-content/uploads/sites/7/2017/01/What-Kids-Are-Reading-2017.pdf on June 23, 2023.

Reynolds, J. (2017). *Long way down.* New York: Simon & Schuster.

Reynolds, P. H. (2003). *The dot.* Cambridge, MA: Candlewick Press.

Reynolds, P. H. (2004). *Ish.* Cambridge, MA: Candlewick Press.

Rhodes, J. P. (2018). *Ghost boys.* New York: Little, Brown Books for Young Readers.

Rhodes-Courter, A. (2008). *Three little words.* New York: Atheneum.

Rhonda, D. (2021, March 20). *How to make a notebook in Canva* [Video]. Accessed at www.youtube .com/watch?v=WUkY9-D5qkw on July 5, 2023.

Richards, C. (2018). *Civic roles in the community: How citizens get involved.* Ada, OK: PowerKids Press.

Rinker, S. D. (2021). *It's so quiet: A not-quite-going-to-bed book.* San Francisco, CA: Chronicle Books.

Rockliff, M. (2016). *Chik chak shabbat* (K. Brooker, Illus.). Cambridge, MA: Candlewick Press.

Roth, V. (2014). *Divergent.* New York: Katherine Tegen Books.

Salem, T. (2018, May 3). *Proximity to books enhances children's learning.* Accessed at www.usnews.com /news/national-news/articles/2018-05-03/proximity-to-books-enhances-childrens-learning on July 5, 2023.

Salinger, J. D. (1951). *The catcher in the rye.* Boston: Little, Brown.

Salwen, K., & Salwen, H. (2010). *The power of half: One family's decision to stop taking and start giving back.* Boston: Houghton Mifflin Harcourt.

Sandler, G., & Howell, S. (n.d.). *7 ways of creating psychological safety for students.* Accessed at www.iste.org/explore/classroom/7-ways-creating-psychological-safety-students on July 5, 2023.

Schaeffer. K. (2021, November 12). *Among many U.S. children, reading for fun has become less common, federal data shows.* Accessed at www.pewresearch.org/short-reads/2021/11/12/among -many-u-s-children-reading-for-fun-has-become-less-common-federal-data-shows on June 23, 2023.

Schmoker, M. (2011). *Focus: Elevating the essentials to radically improve student learning.* Alexandria, VA: Association of Supervision and Curriculum Development.

Senker, C. (2021). *A teen guide to being eco in your community.* Mankato, MN: Capstone Classroom.

Serravallo, J. (2019, October 13). *Effective 5- to 7-minute reading conferences.* Accessed at https://middleweb.com/41336/effective-5-to-7-minute-reading-conferences on April 18, 2023.

Shan, D. (2002) *Cirque du freak: A living nightmare.* Boston: Little, Brown & Company.

Shakespeare, W. (2011). *Romeo and Juliet* (B. A. Mowat & P. Werstine, Eds.). New York: Simon & Schuster. (Original work published 1597)

Sharratt, L., & Fullan, M. (2009). *Realization: The change imperative for deepening district-wide reform.* Thousand Oaks, CA: Corwin.

Simmons, L. (2021, February 14). *Using picture books to engage students in STEM/STEAM.* Accessed at https://mackinlearning.com/using-picture-books-to-engage-in-stem-steam on July 5, 2023.

Simmons, L. (2022, August 16). *3 ways to create a maker culture in your school* [Blog post]. Accessed at https://mackinlearning.com/3-ways-to-create-a-maker-culture-in-your-school on July 5, 2023.

Slater, D. (2017). *The 57 bus.* New York: Farrar, Straus and Giroux.

Smith, A. (n.d.). *9 creative ways to celebrate student success in your classroom* [Blog post]. Accessed at https://teachstarter.com/us/blog/11-ways-to-celebrate-student-success-2 on April 17, 2023.

Smith, D. (2011). *If the world were a village: A book about the world's people.* Toronto, Ontario, Canada: Kids Can Press.

Smith, L. (2021). *Six words gets to the point.* Accessed at https://sixwordmemoirs.com/about on April 17, 2023.

Smith, S. (2021, October 25). *Kansas students stand up to hate, bigotry in push to replace Klan leader's name.* Accessed at https://kansasreflector.com/2021/10/25/kansas-students-stand-up-to-hate-bigotry-in-push-to-replace-klan-leaders-name on April 17, 2023.

Sparks, N. (2014). *The notebook.* New York: Grand Central Publishing.

Spencer, J., & Juliani, A. J. (2017). *Empower: What happens when students own their learning.* Canterbury, England: Impress.

Spires, A. (2014). *The most magnificent thing.* Tonawanda, NY: Kids Can Press.

Staff, T. (2022). *A giant list of really good essential questions.* Accessed at www.teachthought.com/pedagogy/examples-of-essential-questions on July 5, 2023.

Steinbeck, J. (1937). *Of mice and men.* New York: Penguin Books.

Steinbeck, J. (1939). *The grapes of wrath.* New York: Viking Press.

Stevenson, B. (2014). *Just mercy: A story of justice and redemption.* New York: Spiegel & Grau.

Stevenson, R. (2022). *Kid trailblazers: True tales of childhood from changemakers.* Philadelphia, PA: Quirk Books.

Stone, T. (2019). *Girl rising: Changing the world one girl at a time.* Pottsville, PA: Ember.

Stump, S. (2021, October 25). *Paradise football team rises again after California's deadliest fire spared team's field.* Accessed at https://today.com/news/good-news/paradise-football-team-rebuilt-californias-deadliest-fire-spared-teams-rcna3696 on April 17, 2023.

Sundem, G. (2016). *Real kids, real stories, real character: Choices that matter around the world.* Plymouth, MN: Free Spirit Publishing.

Svec, D. (2020, January 14). *Lit at Lunch.* [Conference presentation]. FETC 2020 Conference, Miami, Florida.

Thomas B. Fordham Institute. (2016, September 23). *What are "text sets," and why use them in the classroom?* Accessed at https://fordhaminstitute.org/national/commentary/what-are-text-sets-and-why-use-them-classroom on April 17, 2023.

Tovani, C. (2011). *So what do they really know? Assessment that informs teaching and learning.* Portland, ME: Stenhouse.

Trevino, C. (2021). *Seaside stroll.* Watertown, MA: Charlesbridge Publishing.

Ullmer, C. (2023). *Speed dating books.* Accessed at https://choiceliteracy.com/article/speed-dating-books on June 24, 2023.

United Nations Educational, Scientific and Cultural Organization (UNESCO). (2017, September). *More than one-half of children and adolescents are not learning worldwide.* Accessed at http://uis .unesco.org/sites/default/files/documents/fs46-more-than-half-children-not-learning-en-2017.pdf on April 18, 2023.

University of Nevada, Reno. (2010, May 21). *Books in home as important as parents' education in determining children's education level.* Accessed at www.sciencedaily.com/releases/2010/05 /100520213116.htm on January 3, 2019.

Verde, S. (2018). *Hey, wall: A story of art and community* (J. Parra, Illus.). New York: Simon & Schuster Books for Young Readers.

Walker, B. F. (2012). *Black boy white school.* New York: HarperTeen.

Walters, E. (2005). *Juice.* Victoria, BC, Canada: Orca Book Publishers.

Ward, J. (2017). *Sing, unburied, sing.* New York: Simon & Schuster.

Warren, D. (2023). *The state of pediatric mental health in America 2023 report.* Accessed at www.officepracticum.com/blog/the-state-of-pediatric-mental-health-in-america-2023-report on June 30, 2023.

Watson, A. (2021). *My monster Moofy.* Thomaston, ME: Tilbury House Publishers.

Wexler, N. (2021). *Never heard of Lucy Calkins? Here's why you should have.* Accessed at www.forbes.com /sites/nataliewexler/2021/11/14/never-heard-of-lucy-calkins-heres-why-you-should-have/?sh =7b3c774d2c37 on May 25, 2023.

Wiesel, E. (2012). *Night.* New York: Farrar, Straus and Giroux.

Wiggins, A. (2022, April 1). *The assessment system that made me love grading again (Yes, really!).* Accessed at https://ascd.org/el/articles/the-assessment-system-that-made-me-love-grading-again-yes-really on April 18, 2023.

Wiggins, G. P., & McTighe, J. (2011). *The understanding by design guide to creating high-quality units.* Alexandria, VA: Association of Supervision and Curriculum Development.

Willems, M. (2019). *Because* (A. Ren, Illus.). Westport, CT: Hyperion Press for Children.

Willingham, D. (2015, April 15). Should kids get time to read for pleasure during school? *The Washington Post.* Accessed at https://washingtonpost.com/news/answer-sheet/wp/2015/04/30 /should-kids-get-time-to-read-for-pleasure-during-school on April 18, 2023.

Wolf, M. (2018). *Reader, come home: The reading brain in a digital world* (C. Stoodley, Illus.). New York: Harper.

World Economic Forum. (2023). *The future of jobs report 2023.* Accessed at www.weforum.org/reports /the-future-of-jobs-report-2023 on July 5, 2023.

Yamada, K. (2016). *What do you do with a problem?* (M. Besom, Illus.). Everett, WA: Compendium.

Yoon, N. (2016). *The sun is also a star.* London: Penguin Books.

Yousafzai, M. (2015). *I am Malala: The girl who stood up for education and was shot by the Taliban.* New York: Little, Brown.

Zheng, F. (2022). Fostering students' well-being: The mediating role of teacher interpersonal behavior and student-teacher relationships. *Frontiers in Psychology, 12.* https://doi.org/10.3389/fpsyg .2021.796728

Zoboi, I. (2020). *Black enough: Stories of being young and black in America.* New York: Balzer + Bray.

Index

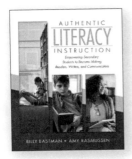

Authentic Literacy Instruction
Billy Eastman and Amy Rasmussen

Imagine a thriving English classroom—one that's active, experiential, collaborative, and rigorous. *Authentic Literacy Instruction* will help you not just imagine this classroom, but also create it. Use the book's doable action plan to reinvigorate your practices and tap into the passions and strengths of every student.

BKF948

Turning the Page on Complex Texts
Diane Lapp, Barbara Moss, Maria C. Grant, and Kelly Johnson

Discover how to select appropriate complex texts and design instruction to meet the needs of every K–12 student.

BKF654

Close Reading in the Secondary Classroom
Jeff Flygare

Learn to effectively teach close-reading skills in middle-school and high-school classrooms. Use literary analysis to increase students' reading comprehension and critical thinking skills.

BKL033

I'm Listening
Beth Pandolpho

Rely on *I'm Listening* to help you drive deeper, more meaningful learning by integrating relationship building into lesson design. Increase student engagement with social-emotional learning to create a positive learning environment.

BKF926